To Kill A President

M. WESLEY SWEARINGEN

TO KILL A PRESIDENT

FINALLY---AN EX-FBI AGENT RIPS ASIDE THE VEIL OF SECRECY THAT KILLED JFK

2008

To Kill A President

CONTENTS

....AND IT CAME TO PASS THAT CAMELOT FADED INTO HISTORY

DISCLAIMER

This manuscript was submitted to the Federal Bureau of Investigation on January 16, 2008, for review, pursuant to the FBI Prepublication Review Policy (PRP) Manual of Administrative Operations and Procedure (MAOP), Part I, 1-24.

By letter dated March 28, 2008, the FBI has concluded that nothing contained in the manuscript fell within a restricted area of disclosure. Therefore, the FBI has no objection to my providing this manuscript, as presented, for publication.

The FBI also stated "that the views expressed in the article do not necessarily represent the views of the FBI."

AUTHOR'S NOTE

In 1978, the FBI raided my attorney's law offices at night without a warrant and seized a 212 page manuscript entitled *FBI CHICANERY*. The manuscript was never returned to me but it ended up as evidence in two different court cases where the FBI lost lawsuits that had been filed against the FBI for wrongdoing.

A few years later I submitted a manuscript to the FBI for prepublication review, which was to have been returned within 30 working days. It was not returned for over a year and not until my attorney Charles R. Garry had requested the FBI to respond to its review. The FBI made several deletions but by then I had lost a book publishing contract.

In 1995, the FBI insisted on yet another prepublication review of the manuscript entitled *FBI SECRETS, An Agent's Exposé*.

This manuscript about JFK was submitted to the FBI in January 2008 for prepublication review. The FBI has ruled that I cannot identify agents below the level of Assistant Special Agent in Charge (ASAC) without their permission or without showing proof that they are deceased even though the agents had violated criminal laws and their oath to defend the Constitution of the United States. So, where I have been unable to locate death certificates for agents with relatively common names, I have used a pseudonym.

This is a work of non-fiction however some scenes or stories may sound more like fiction. I have attempted to stay as close to the factual details as I have remembered them, but with all the cover-up, from various sources, including the FBI and the CIA, it may appear that certain events never happened, or have been distorted. This is not my intent.

In my 25-year career as a Special Agent of the FBI, I discovered that different witnesses see, hear, and recall details differently. This is always prevalent during the interview of witnesses to events such as a bank robbery.

I have not strayed from the known facts surrounding the assassination of President John F. Kennedy, except where I have personal knowledge that the true facts have not been revealed. In some cases, the government has twisted the facts so badly that no one can make sense of the details. However, I learned certain facts as a FBI agent that have convinced me that Lee Harvey Oswald was not the lone assassin as was claimed by the FBI, the Warren Commission, or as others have so proclaimed.

We have seen how both the CIA and the FBI have badly mishandled events and information leading up to the bombing of the Murrah Federal Building in Oklahoma City on April 19, 1995 and the destruction of the World Trade Center in New York City on September 11, 2001.

The bombing of the Murrah Federal Building in Oklahoma City occurring on April 19, 1995 was in direct retaliation for the FBI's catastrophic mishandling of the Branch Davidian standoff in Waco, Texas, from February 28, 1993 to April 19, 1993. The Oklahoma City bombing was the worst terrorist attack in American history, until September 11, 2001, when the fiendish attack, on the World Trade Center towers in New York City and the Pentagon, shocked the world.

If Lee Harvey Oswald was truly a lone assassin why should the government and its various agencies and bureaus withhold any information whatsoever related to the investigation of Kennedy's assassination?

On the other side of the issue of who is guilty for Kennedy's death, it is insulting to the American people for government bureaucrats to think that the public can't handle the truth. The public is made up of the media, professionals such as teachers, doctors, lawyers, merchants, business leaders, entertainers, sportsmen, actresses and actors. Maybe someone with a first grade education can't handle the truth, but do not be condescending and say the voters of America can't handle the truth.

In 1975-1976, during the hearings of the Senate Church Committee and the House Select Committee on Assassinations, Congress saw the danger of the FBI and CIA covering up their nefarious activities to abort the laws and the Constitution of the United States.

I believe the American Government and its investigative agencies are bankrupt. It is scandalous that in this so-called democratic society, after all the official investigations and media inquiries, our government claims it still doesn't know what happened to President Kennedy.

"Time is precious, but truth is more precious than time."

————Disraeli

*To My Wife Patti For Her Love, Understanding, Patience
Through The Tough Scenes And Her Finesse In Editing*

INTRODUCTION

N ow that E. Howard Hunt has died at the age of 88, as of January 23, 2007, it _may_ _be_ _safe_ for me to tell what I know about the conspiracy to assassinate President John F. Kennedy. Hunt was a former CIA agent. He was caught red-handed during the Watergate break-in and he was prosecuted for his part in the Watergate scandal, which resulted in former President Richard M. Nixon resigning to avoid being impeached from office. I am not sure that Hunt was the last of the co-conspirators to depart this world. We shall see.

In my first book, *FBI SECRETS, An Agent's Exposé,* I detailed several instances of FBI corruption and wrongdoing which had been ordered by Hoover, and his bootlicks, such as the wide spread program of Black Bag Jobs, which were illegal searches, and **COINTELPRO**, an acronym for the counter intelligence program. These programs were intended to neutralize individuals and organizations which J. Edgar Hoover disapproved.

In the last chapter of *FBI SECRETS,* I wrote about several lawsuits that had been filed against the FBI. The outcome of some of those cases had not been decided at the time of that publication.

One case that had been decided was the Business and Professional Interests (BPI) case in Chicago. The FBI had lied to Congress and to Judge Kirkland handling the BPI case. The FBI had testified under oath in 1975 that it had conducted only 238 black bag jobs nationwide between the years 1942 to 1966, but when the FBI saw my signed affidavit that I had submitted to the court, the FBI admitted in 1981 that "at least 500 black bag jobs had been conducted in the Chicago area alone directed against approximately fifty targets." The FBI also acknowledged that "if the bag jobs were done today, they would be illegal."

When the BPI won their lawsuit against the FBI, General Counsel Doug Cassel told the media, "Without Wes Swearingen, we never would have won the case."

I did not receive any income from the BPI for helping them win their court case against the FBI, which was all but lost until I furnished affidavits to the court.

Soon after Raymond Wannall, who was then the Assistant Director of the FBI's Intelligence Division, testified before Congress, he visited Los Angeles and told the agents in the Intelligence Division about how the FBI managed to cover up the number of black bag jobs by having agents testify before the Church Committee who knew nothing about black bag jobs.

In January 1978, the Department of Justice released a forty-page report revealing that top FBI officials including J. Edgar Hoover, Clyde Tolson, John P. Mohr, Nicholas P. Callahan, Ivan W. Conrad, Clarence M. Kelley, and G. Speights McMichael (see FBI SECRETS, page 145-146) had wrongfully accepted gratuities, improperly diverted government funds for FBI public relations, and illegally received goods and services.

Federal Judge John F. Grady heard the case in Chicago brought against the FBI and the Chicago police by the relatives of Black Panther Party members Fred Hampton and Mark Clark, who had been gunned down by the Chicago police on December 4, 1969.

I was scheduled to be a witness for the Panthers' relatives in a second trial, the first having ended in a hung jury. The FBI did not want me on the witness stand and they could not afford to let a copy of "FBI CHICANERY" appear before another federal judge as had happened in the BPI case and the Socialist Workers Party cases.

The FBI said that the case would cause hardship to the survivors and that another trial would be expensive for the taxpayers. The FBI was not worried about the expense to the taxpayers and they were not concerned with the feelings of the survivors of the Panthers. The FBI was acting to minimize publicity of allegations that it had conspired with the Chicago police to assassinate members of the Black Panther Party.

In November 1982, Judge Grady nevertheless determined that there was sufficient evidence of a conspiracy between the FBI and the Chicago police to deprive Fred Hampton and Mark Clark of their civil rights to award the plaintiff's $1.8 million in damages.

I did not receive any income from the plaintiffs, or the attorneys for the survivors for my assistance in their winning the case against the FBI and the Chicago police.

Other top FBI officials had lied for 25 years in the wrongful conviction of Elmer Geronimo Pratt, the Los Angeles leader of the BPP who had been convicted in 1972, of a murder he did not commit. In 1997, Pratt was given a hearing in Orange County away from the Los Angeles County that had convicted him. The hearing ended when Pratt was released pending a new trial, which was never held. Pratt sued the FBI and the Los Angeles Police Department (LAPD) and was awarded $4.5 million in 2000.

I did not receive any income from Geronimo Pratt, or his attorneys Stuart Hanlon and the late Johnnie L. Cochran, JR. for my nineteen years of relentless help in their winning the case against the FBI and the LAPD.

Another clear example of the FBI's continued *COINTELPRO*, which the FBI claimed had been discontinued in 1971, was the FBI's involvement in the 1990 bombing of Judy Bari's car while she and Darryl Cherney were inside the car. Bari was a member of Earth First! and she wanted to save the old redwood trees in California. I met with Judy Bari after publication of *FBI SECRETS* and helped her understand hundreds of FBI documents that had been released to her through the Freedom of Information Act (FOIA). We even did a radio talk show together in San Francisco and she helped to set up some book signings. After reading the FOIA documents, I suggested to Bari that in her best interest she could sue the FBI. Bari did sue the FBI, but she died on March 3, 1997, from complications resulting from her bombed-out car. On June 11, 2002, a jury decided that the FBI and the Oakland Police must pay $4.4 million in damages to Daryl Cherney and to the estate of Judy Bari. To my knowledge the FBI has not been charged with the death of Bari in 1997. The FBI definitely tried to kill her in 1990 and they in essence got away with murder.

I did not receive any income from Judy Bari, Daryl Cherney, or their attorneys for helping them win their $4.4 million case against the FBI and the Oakland Police.

The Senate Select Committee studying FBI abuses, also known as the Church Committee, concluded in 1976, "that intelligence activities have undermined the constitutional rights of citizens and that they have done so primarily because checks and balances designed by the framers of the Constitution to assure accountability have not been applied."

I agree with the Church Committee, but really, why should anyone, who truly believes in the Constitution, and who has sworn to protect and defend the Constitution, need a system of checks and balances? If an employee does not know the difference from right and wrong, then they should not be working for the government.

In 1995, the Department of Justice announced that the Office of the Inspector General (OIG) was investigating allegations made by Frederic Whitehurst about corruption in the FBI Laboratory.

J. Edgar Hoover had regularly described the FBI Laboratory in a publicity booklet as "the greatest law enforcement laboratory in the world." Former Assistant Director of the Intelligence Division, William C. Sullivan described the FBI Laboratory as "a real-life counterpart of the busy workroom of the Wizard of OZ—all illusion. Even the famous laboratory files were maintained for show."

In July 2007, US District Judge Nancy Gertner said that the FBI had deliberately withheld evidence in a 1965 murder conviction which sent four innocent men to jail. Two of the men died behind bars. The FBI covered up the injustice for decades. Judge Gertner said, "FBI officials up the line allowed their employees to break laws, violate rules, and ruin lives." Judge Gertner ordered the FBI to pay $101.7 million for the false murder convictions, which is believed to be the largest award of its kind.

The FBI has not apologized for its horrendous deeds.

I believe that when the top-level officials of the FBI are capable of misusing government funds for personal gain, can cover up the assassination of BPP members, condone the imprisonment of innocent men, both black and white, just to protect informants, and can authorize the bombing of Judy Bari's car when she is inside the car, then there is no telling to what extent they would go to cover up the conspiracy to assassinate President John F. Kennedy just to protect their reputations and their lucrative government jobs.

This is my chronological story of various events leading up to the assassination of President John Fitzgerald Kennedy and what happened afterwards in a cover-up. It is my rendition of "what did I know and when did I know it."

CHAPTER 1
Treason in the FBI

Treason is defined in The Random House Dictionary of the English Language as "treason against the sovereign or state." Treason is defined as (1). a. "Violation by a subject of his allegiance to his sovereign or to the state; high treason. B. *U.S.* such a violation directed against the United States, and consisting 'only in levying war against them, or in adhering to their enemies, giving them aid and comfort' " (Constitution of the U.S., III. 3. 1.) (2). *Rare.* "The betrayal of a trust or confidence; breach of faith; treachery."

"Treason is any attempt to impair the well-being of a state to which one owes allegiance; the crime of giving aid or comfort to the enemies of one's government."

In my opinion, anyone who kills the President of the United States is certainly an enemy of the state. A government bureaucracy such as the FBI, which does not bring that person or group of conspirators to justice when such is within their investigative jurisdiction and power, has, for all intents and purposes, committed treason.

I did not expect the FBI to cover up the treasonous act of assassinating President John F. Kennedy. I did not believe, in my wildest thoughts, that the FBI could and would give aid and comfort to the rogue CIA agents, the Chicago Italian Mafia, and certain Cuban exiles, which conspired to kill the President of the United States. I did not believe that the FBI would actually cover up this nefarious deed and thus make itself guilty of treason, but that is exactly what happened.

Since there is no statute of limitations on murder then the constant cover-up of Kennedy's assassination is a continuing treasonous offense being perpetrated by the FBI and the CIA.

To make matters worse, it is the FBI who has primary investigative jurisdiction of treason against the United States. Therefore, to investigate the cover-up of the Kennedy assassination as treason, the FBI would be investigating itself, and everyone knows that will never happen.

The FBI put forth little, if any, effort to identify these men in the CIA who had illegally trained the Mafia and the Cuban exiles, in a secret Florida camp. To my knowledge, the FBI also made no effort to investigate the CIA's illegal training camp in Florida.

J. Edgar Hoover had told William C. Sullivan, Number Three man in the FBI in 1963, that "The thing I am most concerned about...is having something issued so we can convince the public that Oswald is the real assassin."

Sullivan wrote in his book, which was published posthumously, that Hoover directed James H. Gale, who was then an assistant director, exactly what he (Hoover) wanted the results of the assassination inspection to be. Gale, being one of Hoover's sycophants and bootlicks, did exactly what he was told to do. Gale censured two bureau supervisors and transferred them out of Washington. Fifteen others, including Sullivan, were given letters of censure. I worked for Gale when he was Special Agent in Charge (SAC) of the Chicago Division. I know how devious Gale was in order to rise in the FBI. Gale was the Chief Inspector up until Kennedy was assassinated. He should have directed the New Orleans and Dallas offices on how to handle such a person as Lee Harvey Oswald. Oswald was an FBI informant. Inspectors review every informant file during inspections. Why didn't Gale, or his number one man, Mark Felt, make any suggestions to these offices in 1961, 1962, or 1963? Why didn't Gale and Felt mention Oswald to the Director so that Hoover could have made a suggestion? Gale testified that he and Hoover thought Oswald should be on the Security Index, but neither Gale nor Hoover made any suggestions to New Orleans or Dallas.

The FBI is either covering up something, or it was completely out to lunch on the Oswald investigation.

William C. Sullivan, former Assistant Director of the Intelligence Division, was scheduled to testify before the House Committee investigating the assassination of President Kennedy, but before he could testify he was shot to death on July 16, 1978, in an alleged hunting accident. Local authorities claimed that Sullivan had been "mistaken for a deer."

Sullivan had on a bright orange jacket at the time.

J. Edgar Hoover, himself, had a very personal secret, which he took to his grave. Hoover was the first Black FBI agent. Because of his black heritage and his homosexuality, which the CIA reportedly knew about, Hoover could not take the chance of going up against the CIA lest he be crucified by the rogue CIA agents who had participated in a conspiracy to assassinate President John F. Kennedy. Hoover knew that if the CIA could kill Kennedy they could easily embarrass Hoover. Hoover hated to be embarrassed.

CHAPTER 2
Memphis, TN 1951 Hoover Black and Gay

The FBI has instructed me to furnish them with proof of death of the agent I have quoted in this chapter. Since this agent has a very common name and I have no idea when or where he died I will have to use a fictitious name, Agent Joseph, to protect his identity. If the agent is not dead then he would be approximately 107 years old. I am simply following FBI instructions to avoid legal problems.

The FBI had hoped that I might spend the next year attempting to verify Agent Joseph's death to delay publication of this book. I am not falling for their tricks.

Agent Joseph was an old-timer from the early days of J. Edgar Hoover's FBI. Shortly after being assigned to the Memphis FBI office in 1951, fresh out of training school from the FBI's National Academy, I was assigned to work with Agent Joseph who was given the chore of training a rookie. Joseph was a big strapping man just over six feet tall and weighing about 275 pounds. Joseph was much like the actor Sydney Greenstreet in the movie *CASABLANCA* with Humphrey Bogart and Claude Raines. This was before Hoover invented the Weight Program for Special Agents. Joseph first introduced me to the early morning coffee break. Then to the before-lunch coffee break. Then to the after-lunch coffee break and then to the late afternoon coffee break. Surprisingly, Joseph and I did conduct a few interviews during the day. I met many new people. Joseph introduced me to several local police officers and to the police record clerks. I was introduced to officers and clerks at the Shelby County Sheriff's office. I met clerks at the draft board, the credit bureau, the Shelby County Court Clerk's office, and the US Circuit Court Clerk's office. Joseph showed me how to search birth and death records from the monstrous books that were heavy, even for me when I lifted weights to stay in shape. Those records are now reviewed by clicking a computer button.

Joseph was a patient teacher. Joseph taught me the patience for a thorough interview. By the time Joseph ended an interview of a suspect, or a witness, there was nothing more to ask. I owe many thanks to Agent Joseph for his training and his knowledge about the FBI.

Agent Joseph had become a Special Agent of the FBI soon after Hoover was appointed acting director in 1924. However, there were two brothers in the Memphis office who went back to the days before Hoover became the new FBI director. Their first names were Walter and Dewey. They were agents in the original Bureau of Investigation (BI), long before Hoover appeared upon the scene. I met Walter and Dewey, but I never had coffee, or lunch with them. They were their own team of investigators. I was twenty-four, a rookie, just starting a career. They were ready to retire and so there was a huge generation gap. Walter and Dewey, who were both very friendly, were from the old school when FBI agents chased after bank robbers such as "Machine-gun" Kelly and "Baby-face" Nelson with Thompson Sub-machine guns. Walter and Dewey were from the original "Gangbusters" era. They had some interesting stories about Hoover and the FBI.

Walter and Dewey were in what some had called a corrupt Bureau of Investigation. J. Edgar Hoover was supposed to take over and get rid of the corruption. Instead, Hoover became more corrupt than his predecessor in violating the Constitution through ordering illegal searches, ordering assassinations of black leaders, and jailing innocent black leaders. What Joseph told me helped me to understand why Hoover had become America's most notorious racist.

Joseph told me many stories about Hoover and the associate director, Clyde Tolson. I soon learned when Joseph was about to drop a bomb. He would say, "Wes, don't ever tell anyone I told you this, or we'll both be fired."

Joseph's first Hiroshima style bomb was about the sexuality of Hoover and Tolson.

Joseph said, "Wes, don't ever tell anyone I told you this, or we'll both be fired, but the CIA has photos of Edgar and Clyde in a compromising sex act."

I thought Joseph was either nuts, or was pulling my leg because I was the new kid on the block. I shouted, "What?"

Joseph said, "It's true."

"You're joking!"

"It's no joke, Wes."

"I don't believe you."

"You don't have to believe me. In fact I would prefer you didn't believe me. It may stymie your career if you ever tell the wrong person and it gets back to Hoover."

I laughed and slapped my knee like a country boy. "You're pulling my leg!"

Joseph asked, "Why do you think Hoover and Tolson never have any girlfriends?"

"I don't know."

"Why isn't either one of them married?"

"I don't know."

"Why do you think they always have lunch and dinner together?"

I said, "To discuss Communism? I don't know."

"Come on, get real, Wes. No other heads of government bureaus, or agencies, spend that much time together."

I said, "Well, a lot happens in the FBI. Crime never stops."

"No excuse."

I asked, "Are you saying the FBI director and the associate director of the FBI are practicing homosexuals who are hiding in the closet?"

"Yep! The CIA has photos to prove it. But don't tell anyone I told you. I'm coming up for retirement soon."

I thought about what Joseph said. We were told in training school that Hoover and Tolson were inseparable. Various instructors said, with a twinkle in their eyes, that Hoover and Tolson always took vacations together. The two go everywhere together. It was even a sly joke with some instructors who told us about secret trips that Hoover and Tolson made together to a California resort owned by a millionaire with Mafia connections.

Then Joseph added, "And, don't mention it to Walter and Dewey. They will be pissed if they knew I told you. It is like a national secret for them."

Several days went by and then Joseph dropped his Nagasaki style bomb while we were in a bureau car, alone. Joseph always told me stuff about Hoover and Tolson when we were in a bureau car, alone.

Joseph asked, "Wes, did you know that Hoover is part black?"

I turned to Joseph and said, "You are one sick son-of-a-bitch."

Joseph looked at me with a dead pan expression. "It's true."

I asked, "Who the hell told you this crap?"

"Both Walter and Dewey."

"How the hell would they know?"

"They were around before Hoover ever appeared on the scene."

I asked, "So what?"

"So what? So the old Bureau of Investigation boys did a background check on our illustrious J. Edgar Hoover and found that Edgar's natural father was a black man from Mississippi who had had an affair with Edgar's mother."

I said, "Joseph, you need professional help. You have been in the FBI too long. Maybe you need a section eight?"

"Edgar's birth certificate was not filed until several years after he was born. And, then there were alterations to the birth date."

"You mean to tell me somebody from the old Bureau of Investigation actually investigated Hoover?"

Joseph responded, "Yep. Just like I showed you the other day when we were checking birth records at the Bureau of Vital Statistics. You didn't think the old boys club from BI rolled over and played dead when Hoover started chopping off heads did you?"

I said, "Cripes Joseph, being around you is dangerous."

Joseph said, "Not if you keep your mouth shut."

Like the rookie I was, I asked, "If it is true, then why hasn't it ever come out?"

Joseph asked, "Who in their right mind is going to blow the whistle on Hoover who is passing for white?"

"Obviously you're not."

Joseph replied, "Neither will you. Neither will the CIA. Hoover is a master at blackmail. He blackmails presidents, attorneys general, congressmen and senators. If Walter or Dewey ever said anything Hoover would have them for breakfast."

I thought for a minute and then said, "You got that right. Nobody blows the whistle on the old man."

Then Joseph dropped another bomb. "The old Italian gangsters also have pictures of Hoover and Tolson performing sex together. That is why Hoover investigates Communism instead of criminal gangs in Chicago and New York. Hoover doesn't want it known that he is part black, or that he and Tolson are homosexual."

I replied, "I'm beginning to think that working with you is hazardous to my health."

Joseph laughed. "Just forget what I said and you will be okay. Wes, the old expression, 'knowledge is power,' may come in handy some day. You never know when you may need an ace in the hole."

It was more than a half century later when I learned that what Agent Joseph told me was actually the documented truth, which I discuss in the chapter on Millie McGhee Morris.

It should also be noted that the question of Hoover being gay is corroborated by Curt Gentry in his book *J. EDGAR HOOVER: THE MAN AND THE SECRETS*, published by W. W. Norton and Company, Inc., New York, 1991.

It is also noted that the CIA's possession of photographs of Hoover and Clyde Tolson performing oral sex is reported by Anthony Summers in his book *OFFICIAL AND CONFIDENTIAL: The Secret Life of J. Edgar Hoover*, published by G. P. Putman's Sons, New York, 1993.

CHAPTER 3
Chicago, Illinois late 1950s

What I know about the CIA's involvement in the assassination of President John F. Kennedy and the FBI's cover-up of the conspiracy involving the Chicago Mafia and the Anti-Castro Cubans will blow your mind.

The CIA, the Mafia, and the exiled Cubans had the means, motive and the opportunity to assassinate JFK. The late FBI Director, J. Edger Hoover, had the means, motive and opportunity to cover up the assassination.

During the 1950s, I was involved in hundreds of Black Bag Jobs in Chicago along with the late William F. Roemer, Jr., who has written several books about his exploits with the Chicago Mafia. I don't know about Roemer, but sometimes I was asked to do two bag jobs in one day. I also worked in Chicago's Security Division with the late Ralph Hill and the late Marshal "Maz" Rutland. Ralph Hill and I were very good drinking buddies and we shared many of the FBI's top secrets.

Right after Thanksgiving of 1957, Roemer, Hill, and Rutland volunteered to be transferred to the Top Hoodlum Program (THP) from the Security Division. All three were accepted. They had all asked me to volunteer, but I had learned from my Navy experience that you never volunteer for anything lest you get shafted.

Up until November 14, 1957, when a New York state police trooper had discovered a secret organized crime convention in Apalachin, New York, Hoover had denied there ever was any organized crime, Mafia, or La Cosa Nostra. (LCN).

The terms Mafia and La Cosa Nostra were handles invented by law enforcement to add color and to describe the crime families from Italy and Sicily.

Within days of the Apalachin event, Hoover decreed that almost three percent of the Chicago agent personnel would look into this new phenomenon known as the Mafia. Chicago spared only 10 agents from Hoover's onslaught against Communism while the other squads usually had 20 to 22 agents assigned to a squad. Roemer, Hill, and Rutland told me they were assigned one case each. Other agents in the office had 20 cases each. Roemer, Hill, and Rutland said they had obtained the names of important criminals from the daily newspapers. The new supervisor flipped a coin to see which Mafia wise guy would be investigated first. Roemer was given Gussie Alex. Ralph Hill was assigned Sam Giancana. Rutland worked on a mistress of gangster Frank "Strongy" Ferraro who fixed politicians, judges, and public officials.

Richard B. Ogilvie was the chief of the Attorney General's Midwest Office on Organized Crime. He later became sheriff of Cook County and then some years later became governor of Illinois. Ogilvie had described the FBI's Top Hoodlum Program (THP) as "outmoded in its operations."

The truth is that the FBI never had any mode of operation against organized crime until after November 1957. The first mode then was to read the newspapers. The second mode was for Roemer to play handball at a West Side YMCA. The third mode was Ralph Hill's modus operandi to cruise Rush Street restaurants and bars for good food and fast women.

Roemer told me that he did not have the vaguest idea what the Mafia was all about, or what organized crime had been in Chicago other than what he read in the Chicago newspapers. Roemer said he spent days on end in the Chicago Tribune newspaper morgue reading about crime in Chicago. This is a true confession from some of Hoover's finest. Roemer, Hill, and Rutland all said the FBI had a lot of catch up to do because of Hoover's years of self denial.

Ralph Hill decided that the best way to catch up to the fast track was to "interview" the mob bosses girl friends. Hill had a way with women having spent some time working prostitution rings in Chicago. We in Chicago referred to the case classification of 31 as the "pussy posse." Ralph Hill was a very smooth operator.

The bag jobs that Roemer and I did together were illegal searches of the homes and offices of Communist Party members, who, according to Hoover, were planning to overthrow America by force and violence. It never happened, not because of what Hoover's FBI had done, but because of the fact that the Soviet Union fell apart.

Because the illegal bag jobs were so highly confidential, Roemer and I, along with other agents, shared some of the FBI's most guarded secrets. Hoover considered us to be a special breed. Hoover often gave us letters of commendation, sort of a badge of honor, for our illegal accomplishments. When Hoover was feeling generous with the taxpayer's money, he gave us monetary awards of several hundred dollars. Some awards involved a few thousand dollars, which was a hefty sum in the 1950s for performing illegal acts in violation of the Constitution.

During the Senate Select Committee hearings in 1975 and 1976, chaired by Senator Church, black bag jobs were euphemistically referred to by top FBI officials as "surreptitious entries," a more politically correct term than illegal burglaries performed by FBI agents.

While still in Chicago in 1957, when Roemer, Hill, and Rutland were planning new careers, so to speak in fighting organized crime, I investigated the Nationalist Party of Puerto Rico (NPPR).

Some members of the NPPR had shot up the United States Congress in 1954, and so they were considered *the* terrorist group of that time period.

I had developed an informant whom I shall call "Jose" who was a Puerto Rican. FBI rules prohibit me from using informant's names even though they may have been exposed in open court, or in open testimony before the Church Committee.

Jose had been prosecuted for his association with the NPPR group that shot up Congress in 1954. After Jose was paroled for good conduct he was approached to see whether he may have changed while in prison. Everyone deserves a second chance. Right?

Jose appeared to be cooperative. He began to furnish information of value and so I depended more and more upon Jose for information as to what the NPPR had in mind for the near future.

I enjoyed my new found Spanish language work and so I began to study Spanish with records and books from the Linguaphone Institute of London, England. The Spanish was the high class Castilian. Later, I attended a Berlitz school at my own expense and on my own time. The instructor was amazed that I did not have an American accent.

With my knowledge of Spanish and black bag jobs, the late Joseph M. Culkin, who was then my supervisor and with whom I had conducted hundreds of black bag jobs, wanted to keep me in Chicago and so he wrote to Hoover that my performance in Chicago was outstanding and that I had performed my Spanish speaking assignments in an exemplary manner.

About that same time a young guerilla fighter from the Oriente Province of Cuba was fighting his way out of the jungle on his way to Havana, Cuba. In 1959, this guerilla fighter proclaimed himself the dictator of Cuba, tossing out Fulgencio Batista and the organized crime members from the United States who controlled the casinos. His name is Fidel Castro.

I had been watching Castro's every move while working Cuban foreign counterintelligence. I had developed several good informants; one of the best was Ramon, with the help of the late Michael G. Simon, who was another drinking buddy. It was Simon who got me away from Ralph Hill's gin martinis. Working with Simon made me a confirmed scotch drinker.

Culkin was happy with my Cuban work until one day in 1960 I told Culkin that Ramon, a Cuban Exile, had told me about the CIA's training camp in Florida where the CIA was training members of the Chicago Mafia how to kill people, namely Fidel Castro. I also told Culkin about the CIA's plan to invade Cuba at the Bay of Pigs.

Culkin snapped back at me like a caged wild animal. He said, "The CIA does not operate in the United States! It is illegal for the CIA to have a training camp in Florida! Your informant is crazy! Or, maybe both of you are nuts? The U.S military invades countries, not the CIA! I don't have time for this bullshit, Swearingen!"

Culkin probably thought, "Here Swearingen goes again." It was just months earlier that Jose, a Puerto Rican informant, had told me that the NPPR had a plan to kill J. Edger Hoover.

I spent countless hours of overtime working on the NPPR. As it turned out, Jose was feeding me a line of falsehoods about the NPPR wanting to kill Hoover. There was no plot to kill FBI Director J. Edgar Hoover. Culkin did not want a repeat of the NPPR fiasco since he had told Hoover what a great job I had been doing in Chicago.

I will have to admit that I did not believe Ramon, the Cuban-exile informant, when he said the CIA had a training camp in Florida and that the CIA was training the Mafia how to assassinate people. If anything, I thought it should have been the other way around. The Mafia should have been training the CIA how to kill people, or so I thought. I had no idea then that the CIA had such a fantastic group of cold blooded killers at their beck and call.

I had no idea that the CIA was as utterly idiotic as to try to invade Cuba at the Bay of Pigs. I carried a map of Cuba with me when I interviewed exiles who had fled for their lives, often with only the clothes on their backs. When Ramon pointed out the Bay of Pigs on the map I nearly died laughing. I thought for nearly an hour that Ramon must have thought I had just fallen off a turnip truck if he thought I was going to believe such a ridiculous story as an invasion at the Bay of Pigs to take back Cuba, which he claimed was being organized by the CIA.

The more Ramon talked about CIA boats, the CIA planes, the CIA this and the CIA that, the harder I laughed. And then finally, when I could not take any more of his bullshit I got mad and I ordered Ramon out of the car. No one, especially the CIA, could be as dumb as the picture being painted by Ramon for the CIA's invasion of Cuba.

Fidel Castro had fought his way down the mountains from Oriente Province to become the dictator of Cuba and now some rag tag outfit being led by the CIA was going to take back Cuba starting at the Bay of Pigs.

Please, give me a break. No one can be that dense, or brainless. I found out many years later that Ramon was correct. Ramon was part of the ill fated invasion. Luckily he managed to escape alive.

CHAPTER 4
The Planned Bay of Pigs 1960

Chicago, Illinois, 1960.

A Cuban exile, the one known as "Ramon," had called the FBI complaint desk in 1959 and had asked to speak to an agent who knows something about Cuba. John, the complaint agent for that day, referred Ramon to me since I was assigned Cuban intelligence matters in Chicago. Ramon and I talked for a few minutes and then we ended our conversation on friendly terms. Ramon had nothing startling to tell me in 1959 that I did not already know from talking to other Cuban exiles.

Then in May of 1960, Ramon called again and we set up a time and place to meet. Since I was the only agent in Chicago working Spanish language matters at that time, I usually worked alone. The Chicago FBI office supposedly had no one else who could speak Spanish. I met Ramon this day thinking that he most likely had some miscellaneous information about Cuba which may be in the local newspapers. The Chicago papers had daily stories about the newly self-appointed dictator Fidel Castro.

It was a beautiful spring day in Chicago as I drove to the West side of town. Nearly every day is a beautiful day after a long and brutal winter of sloppy snow and soot covered slush in the streets. As I pulled up to the corner of the designated location, a short man built like a hand grenade was waiting on the corner. He spotted the bureau car with no problem. Nearly all FBI cars looked like Chicago four-door police cars with the telltale spotlight and no chrome trim.

For the sake of this trusted Cuban's identity and for the sake of his family, I cannot reveal his true name or describe his physical appearance any further because it would be a dead giveaway to the CIA. No pun intended. However, Ramon was short and stocky. He looked as though he could lick his weight in wildcats. Ramon spoke fluent English with a Cuban accent. He apparently had had a good education. Ramon had a truckload of street smarts. He could tell some fairly wild stories about Cuba that would stand your hair on end.

After introducing ourselves, I drove to a small park where we could talk without being observed by nosey neighbors looking out their apartment windows ready to call the police because two men are sitting in a car in front of their residence. This has happened to me on surveillance.

Ramon began to tell me about the CIA's training camp in Florida. I thought he was nuts and I told him so. I did not have time for a bullshit story.

I said, "It is illegal for the CIA to operate within the United States borders."

Ramon must have thought I was a nitwit. He laughed and said, "Señor, the CIA has a training camp on a Florida university campus." Ramon told me about the training facilities and I thought Ramon was becoming crazier by the minute. Ramon told me about the planned Bay of Pigs invasion in an attempt to overthrow Fidel Castro long before it had happened. The planned invasion was supposedly the brainchild of the CIA. I thought then that Ramon was as nutty as they come possibly needing some professional help. His information about the

CIA plans for the Bay of Pigs invasion made the CIA look so stupid that I had actually ordered Ramon out of the car only after he had told me about the CIA's boats, airplanes, and endless supplies of military equipment. The whole idea of the CIA invading Cuba to get rid of Castro was utterly ridiculous, ludicrous and preposterous—so I thought.

The following year proved that I was the nutty one.

I had routinely interviewed Cubans after examining their 'orange' cards at the Immigration and Naturalization Service (INS). Consequently, I interviewed many Cubans. Except for Ramon, none of them had told me about the CIA training camp in Florida.

Every Cuban I talked to gave me some new information that I did not have previously. As a result, I helped many Cubans find jobs in Chicago and I became a trusted friend. One Cuban informant even invited me to his house to have dinner with his family. I was honored.

Many years' later government documents were released under the Freedom of Information Act (FOIA) indicating that the CIA actually:

1-Did have a secret training camp in Florida, known as JM/Wave.
2-Did have a small navy.
3-Did have planes ready to bomb Cuba.
4-Did back the landing of Cuban exiles at the Bay of Pigs, albeit without the support of President Kennedy, which he originally approved and told the CIA he would support.

CHAPTER 5
The CIA's Bay of Pigs Debacle 1961

What Ramon told me in 1960, which I thought was the most idiotic plan I had ever heard, actually happened. I have heard many goofy stories, but this one took the cake.

In April 1961, the CIA's dream to invade Cuba and dethrone Fidel Castro was the greatest debacle of all time. CIA agent E. Howard Hunt must have been beside himself with excitement. Other CIA agents such as David Sanchez "El Indio" Morales and William Harvey must have gone ballistic.

Senator John F. Kennedy knew the only way into the White House was to ride Hoover's fight against "commonism," as Edgar used to pronounce communism. Soon after Kennedy sat down in the Oval Office he became obsessed with the Communist dictator Fidel Castro.

President Eisenhower had thought of a plan to neutralize Castro, but nothing constructive was done before he turned over the seat of government to Kennedy. On January 3, 1961, about two weeks before Kennedy took office, Eisenhower broke off diplomatic relations with Cuba. Various CIA attempts to kill Castro had failed. On January 30, 1961, President Kennedy declared that communist domination in this hemisphere "can never be negotiated." The CIA knew Kennedy was hot to trot and that they had a big fish on the hook ready to reel in for dinner and so they came up with a plan, which Kennedy promised he would back.

The CIA bought planes, boats, ammunition, and landing craft with the taxpayer's money and the drug money they had stashed away. You name it; the CIA bought it with pictures of George Washington. The Bay of Pigs plan was going like Gangbusters, but then all hell broke loose.

Senate Foreign Relations Chairman William Fulbright, upon learning of plans for the proposed invasion, sent a scorching memorandum to the White House that said if American forces were drawn into battle in Cuba:

> *"We would have undone the work of thirty years in trying to live down earlier interventions...to give this activity even covert support is of a piece with the hypocrisy and criticism for which the United States is constantly denouncing the Soviet Union in the United Nations and elsewhere. This point will not be lost on the rest of the world nor on our own consciences. And remember always, the Castro regime is a thorn in the side but not a dagger in the heart."*

Kennedy puckered after reading Fulbright's memorandum. John realized that the CIA had duped him. Kennedy declined to commit American troops just as the CIA's Operation Mongoose began to fall apart. Talk about an insult. This was like an Englishman's old-fashioned slap in the face with a pair of gloves. The CIA and the Cuban Exiles were devastated. Approximately 1,200 men were captured on the beach. Approximately 90 men were killed.

Kennedy had managed to piss off the CIA, the Cuban Exiles, and the Italian Mafia all in one felled swoop.

Kennedy was so embarrassed over the Bay of Pigs that he fired long-time CIA Director Allen W. Dulles, Deputy Director Charles P. Cabell, and the one mainly responsible for the invasion, Deputy Director Richard Bissell. Kennedy publicly took responsibility for the failure, but privately he blamed the CIA.

The controversial Inspector General's report concluded that ignorance, incompetence, and arrogance on the part of the CIA were responsible for the fiasco.

In the real world one should know better than to turn your back on a group of rogue CIA agents and to fire their bosses who have sanctioned killings around the world.

It is my opinion that a few rogue agents in the CIA had deemed this insult worthy of a duel with their choice of weapons.

It is also my opinion, based upon the live sources that I have interviewed, and the FBI documents I have read, that rogue agents of the CIA, who had trained Cuban exiles and members of the Italian Mafia in Chicago, Miami, New Orleans, and Dallas, to kill Fidel Castro, did as a result of Kennedy's failure to support the Bay of Pigs invasion, turn their anger against their own President and thereby committed treason against the United States by engaging in a conspiracy to assassinate President John F. Kennedy.

CHAPTER 6
Johnny Roselli

In 1940, FBI Director J. Edgar Hoover sent a group of his best FBI agents to Central and South America under the name of the Special Intelligence Service (SIS). President Franklin D. Roosevelt had authorized the FBI to establish a Special Intelligence Service to counter German Nazi intelligence efforts during World War II. Hoover dreamed of expanding the FBI's jurisdiction all over the world. Conducting spy operations was a way to accomplish that dream. However, after World War II, President Harry S. Truman coordinated the federal foreign intelligence activities in a Presidential Directive dated January 22, 1946, which established the Central Intelligence Agency, now known the world over as the CIA.

Soon after the war, however, many of Hoover's finest in the SIS, capitalizing on their language abilities, decided to join the CIA, which irritated Hoover. Robert Maheu was one of the FBI defectors. After having established his contacts through the CIA, Maheu became a private investigator and was then hired by millionaire Howard Hughes. Maheu formed friendships with various gangsters in Las Vegas, including Johnny Roselli, who was the Las Vegas and Hollywood representative of the Chicago mob boss, Sam Giancana. As a young punk, Roselli had been Giancana's hit man.

Johnny Roselli was sent to Hollywood in 1940 to worm his way into the Motion Picture Producers Association, which he did. Three years later Roselli and six other thugs, who had taken over the International Alliance of Theatrical Stage Employees, were indicted and convicted for selling labor peace to the major movie studios. Roselli did several years of hard time.

In the 1950s, Robert Maheu became the liaison between the CIA and the Chicago Mob, known as the Outfit, and was instrumental in setting up the Outfit and the CIA in an attempt to assassinate Fidel Castro. By 1958, Roselli and Maheu were working buddies. Roselli met frequently with Maheu in Las Vegas and Miami. Maheu set the stage for Roselli and the CIA to do their covert dirty work.

According to Ramon, the CIA mounted a massive guerilla-training program in the Florida everglades. The CIA trained Roselli, Giancana, Richard Cain and other gunmen, in the art of assassination, which none of them hardly needed. Johnny Roselli and Sam Giancana had assassinated dozens of mob figures long before they had ever met a CIA agent. Their hits were always on people they knew, individuals they could get close to with a .22 caliber handgun. Using a silencer, they then squeezed off a round or so in the victim's brain. Assassinating the President in the open, surrounded by hundreds, maybe thousands of onlookers and TV cameras needed extensive practice and planning. This is where the CIA entered the scene. Roselli, Giancana, and their henchmen were trained with special CIA Task Force weapons using ammunition that exploded upon impact. This training and the special weapons developed by the CIA were supposed to be used against Fidel Castro. The attempts to kill Castro failed because Castro's counterintelligence unit was superior to anything the CIA and the Outfit could muster.

There is some evidence to support the theory that the CIA used the Outfit including Giancana, and Johnny Roselli in particular, to kill President John F. Kennedy.

Ramon told me in 1961 that Sam Giancana and Johnny Roselli had been working with the CIA in an attempt to get rid of Fidel Castro. Ramon also said Richard Cain was part of the CIA's training team in Florida. I went to Bill Roemer and asked him what he knew about Giancana, Roselli, and Cain working with the CIA. Roemer just laughed and said, "Wes, if Sam Giancana or his hit men, Johnny Roselli and Cain, were working with the CIA, I'd be the first to know."

I spoke to Ralph Hill and Ralph gave me essentially the same answer. Although Ralph Hill was honest enough to admit that he hardly knew what Giancana was doing at that time. I had to assume that Ramon may have been pulling my chain.

Roemer later admitted that Bob Maheu, the former FBI and CIA agent, who worked for Howard Hughes in Las Vegas, had set up meetings with the CIA and Sam Giancana, Johnny Roselli, and Santo Trafficante, the Mafia boss in Miami, Florida. Roemer admits that he saw Roselli as the only one serious about knocking off Fidel Castro. Roemer does not explain when he thought this to be the case. He had told me in 1962 that he did not know the Mafia was working with the CIA to get Fidel Castro.

It would have been nice had William F. Roemer Jr. listened to what Ramon was saying from 1960 to October 1962. It might just have been possible for the FBI to throw a monkey wrench into the plans of a few rogue CIA agents. It may just have been possible for the FBI to have stopped the assassination of President John F. Kennedy.

Johnny Roselli had been subpoenaed before the Senate Intelligence Committee in May 1975, where he testified behind closed doors. Roselli allegedly gave the Church Committee "a good deal of information."

Roselli's former mob boss, Sam Giancana, was scheduled to testify but he was found dead on June 19, 1975, just days before his scheduled appearance.

Johnny Roselli was scheduled to appear again before the Church Committee. Roselli missed his second appointment to testify. His disfigured body was found on August 7, 1976, stuffed into an oil drum in Dumbfoundling Bay near Miami, Florida.

After I retired and became a whistleblower, a reliable source in Hollywood, who requested anonymity, advised me that Roselli bragged to the source, who was a made man in the La Cosa Nostra, that Roselli had shot at and may have killed John Kennedy. After Lee Harvey Oswald fired the first shot at the President's limousine, creating panic and hysteria, Roselli and his men then finished the job from the sewer drain and the grassy knoll while the police and witnesses were running around like chickens with their heads cut off.

It should be noted that two other independent sources unknown to the Mafia made man had advised me years later in 2004 that Richard Cain had been present on the Grassy Knoll at the time of the shooting of President Kennedy.

It is interesting to note that Johnny Roselli contacted his old CIA handler; Colonel Sheffield Edwards on May 12, 1966, just two and a half years after Kennedy was assassinated. Colonel Edwards had retired from the CIA and had opened a security firm named Sheffield Edward's Associates, 1815 H Street, N. W., Washington, D.C. This was apparently a panic meeting.

Two FBI agents approached Johnny Roselli on the streets of Los Angeles and said they wanted to talk to him about a matter of National Security. Roselli was a hard-core Mafia hit man who was used to whacking family members. He had broken arms, legs, fingers, even busted knee caps of welshers who didn't ante up to the mob.

Just picture this. Two of Hoover's faceless empty suits walk up to Roselli on a beautiful spring day in Los Angeles, flash their FBI credentials, and say they want to talk to Roselli on a matter of National Security. You and I know the Mafia is used to being approached by FBI types for an interview, so there should have been no sweat on Roselli's part. When Roselli's boss, Sam Giancana, was approached by at least eight armed FBI agents at O'hare International Airport in 1961, with Bill Roemer taking verbal jabs at Giancana, Sam called the FBI agents a bunch of "cocksuckers." This is the typical Mafia reaction. They tell the FBI to "fuck off" or "kiss my ass." Giancana said to Roemer, in front of many travelers, "Suck my dick, you cocksucker." This is what Roemer bragged about to me, personally, on many different occasions. Roemer loved it.

This is not what Roemer reported in his FD-302 Interview Report form to Hoover. Roemer admitted that he did not report the whole text of Sam Giancana's interview to Hoover. So, Roemer admitted he lied to Hoover. If Roemer could lie to Hoover then Roemer could certainly lie to me about not knowing Roselli, Giancana, and Cain were involved in the killing of President Kennedy. However, Roemer did tell me what Giancana actually said at the airport, several times, as though it was one of the exciting events in Roemer's life.

What does Roselli do after being contacted by two FBI agents? He hops a plane to Washington, D.C., with his attorney, and makes a bee-line for Colonel Edward's office. Actually Roselli met in a neighborhood bar near Edward's office where he could grab a quick drink. According to Roselli's former CIA handler and babysitter, Roselli, who could normally handle a few cocktails, barely touched his drink. Roselli was out of his wits and scared to death that Sam Giancana would find out that two FBI agents had approached Roselli on the street. That is a joke. Roselli could have been on "Saturday Night Live."

It does not make sense that Roselli would be afraid that Giancana, or anyone else, would hear that Roselli had been approached by two FBI types. To hear Roemer tell it, the FBI approached some mob member every time a gangster turned around. Roselli was afraid only because he thought that the FBI had the goods on him and could connect him to the Kennedy assassination. With Richard Cain on the Grassy Knoll and Roselli in the sewer, Cain, who was Roemer's top informant, could have fingered Roselli for the hit on President Kennedy, and Roselli knew it. There is no other explanation for Roselli to have flown from Los Angeles to Washington D.C. to meet with his former CIA handler, so nervous that he could not finish his drink. We are talking about a Mafia hit man being afraid of two faceless FBI agents politely asking for permission to talk to Roselli. Let's get real folks.

What did Giancana do when Bill Roemer kept harassing Sam in public? Giancana filed a harassment suit against Roemer and the FBI which Giancana won.

What did Roselli do when approached by two FBI agents? Roselli panicked because he thought he had been caught by Hoover's FBI.

Within a few months Johnny Roselli had a Washington power broker, attorney Edward P. Morgan, spread the word to columnist Jack Anderson that Fidel Castro and the communists had killed Kennedy. Roselli had pulled off the greatest coup d'etat since his part in the conspiracy in the well orchestrated assassination plot to kill President John F. Kennedy. Once

Anderson's column landed on the streets in "The Washington Merry-go-round," it exploded like a political H-bomb. Instead of the focus being on Castro and Cuba, the Church Committee became more interested in the CIA's connections to Organized Crime. This caused the committee to lose sight of their objective in determining who killed Kennedy. In lieu of finding a conspiracy the committee spent the majority of its resources spinning its wheels in the muck and mire churned up by the CIA. The CIA refused to give the Church Committee the time of day.

In support of the true assassins, and continuing the debilitating smoke screen, the Chicago Mob blamed Castro and the communists for Kennedy's murder. Bill Roemer, one of the Chicago agents listening to the Chicago mobsters over FBI bugs, and not understanding a word of Italian, just laughed and went about punching the bag at the YMCA on Chicago's West Side. Sometimes Roemer acted as though the bag had punched him more times than he had punched the bag.

With all of the years I spent investigating the Communist Party in Chicago, I never found CP members guilty of anything but possibly overtime parking and that was not often. There is no way the Communist Party could have been behind the Kennedy assassination with top leaders of the Communist Party such as Gus Hall, Morris Childs, and Jack Childs in control of what was happening in the CP. All three men were informants for the FBI. I can assure you that the FBI and the Communist Party were not part of the assassination. However, the FBI was a part of the conspiracy cover-up which I consider treason. That is a whole different ball game.

Why in the world would a big-time smooth operator like Johnny Roselli bother to put the blame on Fidel Castro for the Kennedy assassination when FBI Director J. Edgar Hoover had already declared Lee Harvey Oswald the lone assassin just days after JFK had been murdered—unless Roselli truly was at Dealey Plaza and truly did take a shot at Kennedy? Roselli was guilty as hell and he knew it. Roselli did not know whether the FBI knew it and so he had to spread the word that someone else had killed Kennedy just to keep the heat off his own back.

In my opinion, anyone such as Vincent Bugliosi, Oliver "Buck" Revell, W. Mark Felt, Clarence Kelley and others who cannot understand what Johnny Roselli was attempting to do simply does not comprehend the mentally of a con artist, or, for reasons unknown, these individuals are awkwardly attempting to cover up the CIA's twisted resolve to kill President John F. Kennedy.

CHAPTER 7
Sam Giancana

Sam Giancana was born May 28, 1908, in Chicago's Little Italy, a neighborhood known as the Patch, and was christened Momo Jimmy Salvatore Giancana. His father called him Mo. A half century later the FBI used the code name "MO" for one of its wiretaps on a mob business. The Italian foreigners who settled in the Patch were largely from Sicily.

When Sam's mother died in 1910 from a miscarriage, Sam's father, a traditional macho Italian male soon remarried. It was not a happy marriage and Sam grew up seeing and hearing his father abuse his stepmother. His father often used Sam as a punching bag. Sam's father believed that the best way to tame an unruly brat was to beat the hell out of him.

The beatings had just the opposite effect. Sam became a hopeless excuse for a kid and by the time he was ten he was sent to the St. Charles Reformatory. Sam was released after six months in the reformatory but he did not return home. Instead, he wondered the streets of Chicago, much like a homeless person, sleeping in abandoned cars and cardboard boxes. Sam stole food during the day from local Italian delis and pizzerias. He soon joined a street gang. The gang's petty crimes became boring and Sam turned to stealing cars. When car theft bored Sam, he turned to murder. In no time at all Sam Giancana became the meanest, most vicious punk kid anywhere in Chicago. By age thirteen he had become a sleazy misfit.

As Sam grew older he became interested in women. When there were no girls around for the boys to gang bang, they had what they called "pulling parties." Sam and his misfits got together and masturbated. They had contests to see who could ejaculate first and shoot their sperm farthest. According to my friends and fellow FBI agents, Bill Roemer and Ralph Hill, who investigated Sam Giancana and the Chicago Outfit, Giancana was a totally demented whoremonger and scum bag.

By 1957, Sam Giancana had become the Boss of Chicago's underworld, known as the Outfit. It is no wonder that FBI agent William F. Roemer Jr. hated Sam Giancana with a passion. Giancana represented everything Bill Roemer despised.

Sam Giancana was shot to death in his own home on June 19, 1975, just before he was to testify before Congress.

Dominic 'Butch' Blasi, Giancana's bodyguard, appointment secretary, driver, and confidant, for nearly thirty years, was the only person, observed, entering Sam's house in Oak Park, Illinois, that night after Sam's guests had departed. The only other persons in the house were Joe DePersio and his wife, who were in another room watching the Johnny Carson Show while Sam cooked up some of his favorite Italian sausage in his private kitchen.

The intelligence unit of the Chicago police had watched Sam's house but then allegedly ended the tail after the guests went home. They did not see the killer enter the house, or so they claim.

Sam Giancana was hit at close range with a High-Standard Duromatic lightweight .22 caliber handgun with a silencer. The murder was professional. The killer had shot seven times, all at point-blank range, all to the head, first to the back of the head, then under the chin, and in the mouth. Sam never knew what hit him. Sam didn't give his victims a chance to run so why should Sam's killer be any different? The killer was surely Giancana trained.

Sam's body was discovered later that night by his house keeper and caretaker, Joe DePersio. Giancana was sprawled on the kitchen floor. The weapon, strangely enough, was found along the side of the road on the route to Butch Blasi's home. Even stranger was the fact that Blasi was never charged with the murder. It was almost as though the law enforcement authorities, including Bill Roemer of the FBI, wanted Sam Giancana dead, but did not want to prosecute anyone for fear that the CIA's relationship to Sam would be revealed in court.

Roemer quite possibly pushed the prosecutor's office not to pursue Giancana's murder for fear that Richard Cain would have been exposed as an FBI Top Hood informant who had participated in the assassination of President Kennedy. The lack of prosecution could not have been from fear that it was a mob killing. The FBI knew that some police officers were on the take.

Bill Roemer said he did not believe Butch Blasi did the shooting. This is easy for Roemer to say when he considered Blasi a pocket informant in 1962. Some others believed that Butch Blasi might have introduced the killer(s) to Sam Giancana. How naïve can one be? There was no information that Butch had returned to Sam's home with a friend. Sam Giancana knew too much and the CIA and the mob wanted Sam dead. If Blasi did not shoot Giancana then Blasi most certainly knew who did. Roemer was not about to say that Blasi shot Giancana because Roemer knew that the CIA would kill Roemer and Blasi if Roemer said anything about the JFK murder and the Giancana/CIA connection.

Bill Roemer, who died of lung cancer at age 69 in 1996, was truly naïve. Roemer had once heard Sam Giancana over FBI bugs talking to a Mafia friend about Sam sleeping with Marilyn Monroe. Bill told me that Marilyn Monroe was sleeping with black men. Bill said that he heard Sam ask his friend, "You like fucking the same broad the brothers are fucking?"

When Bill Roemer told me that Marilyn Monroe was sleeping with some blacks, I said to Bill, "The brothers are not black men. Giancana is talking about the brothers Bobby and John Kennedy." Roemer was speechless. After a few seconds he replied, "Jesus Christ!" This was the only time I recall Roemer ever using profanity.

Bill Roemer was a racist. His first thought, after hearing the word "brothers" over the FBI's wiretap, was to think of the "N" word and that Marilyn Monroe was sleeping with blacks. What difference did it make if she had slept with black men? Roemer, of course, thought this was a mortal sin and he could not bear the thought of the President and the Attorney General of the United States having sex with the same woman that members of the Mafia were pillowing.

This, of course, did not bother Ralph Hill or Marshall Rutland. They would have balled Monroe if they had had the chance.

Ralph Hill was the case agent on Sam Giancana, which meant in FBI terms, that Hill was responsible for developing information on Giancana and for writing investigative reports. Ralph Hill knew everything about Sam Giancana that the FBI knew anywhere in the world. Ralph and I were good friends, what some might call drinking buddies. Ralph regularly told me stories about Sam Giancana, Johnny Roselli, Bobby and John Kennedy, Frank Sinatra, Marilyn Monroe, and many others, whose names fade into a menagerie of perverted sex stories, assassination targets, and underworld double-dealing and double-crossing. Ralph Hill had more horror stories about celebrity, Mafia, and presidential sex than you could shake a stick at.

Ralph Hill knew many of the sex stories about Sam Giancana and his friends because Ralph developed many of the Mob's girl friends such as Judy Campbell and Darlene Caifano as informants after Ralph had had sex with them.

Richard Cain was shot to death in 1973.

Sam Giancana was shot to death in 1975.

Johnny Roselli was butchered in 1976.

CHAPTER 8
Richard Cain

<u>Richard Cain was a quadruple agent.</u>

Cain was a Chicago cop who had worked for Sam Giancana collecting hush money to pay off Chicago's big wig police officers. Richard Cain also worked for the CIA recruiting some of Chicago's tough guys for training at the CIA's JM/Wave camp in Florida.

Now, for the real kicker—Bill Roemer claims that Richard Cain was one of his top THP informants.

So, according to Bill Roemer, who falsely claims to have been one of Hoover's hand-picked agents for the THP squad, Richard Cain was:

1- A Chicago cop.
2- Sam Giancana's right-hand man.
3- A CIA asset.
4- A FBI informant, whom Roemer considered good enough to be classified as a Special Agent of the FBI.

It is no wonder that Bill Roemer loudly proclaimed to the world that Lee Harvey Oswald was the lone assassin who killed President John F. Kennedy. If Roemer had released so much as a peep to the Warren Commission that Richard Cain and Johnny

Roselli were involved in the Kennedy assassination, Roemer's career and his life would have been terminated immediately.

Bill Roemer once said that as long as Cain did not tell Roemer what he, Cain, did, was doing, or what he was about to do, such as conspire with Sam Giancana, Johnny Roselli and the CIA to kill Fidel Castro, or President Kennedy, it was okay with Roemer. Can you imagine Roemer not asking Cain about the CIA and the plot to kill Kennedy after I asked Roemer if he knew anything about Giancana, Cain, and Roselli being involved with the CIA?

Richard Cain and Bill Roemer were the best of buddies according to Roemer's own words. Because of the secret agreement Roemer and Cain had made, Cain was not obligated in any way to tell Roemer anything about whether he, Cain, had assisted in killing Kennedy. As a Top Echelon informant, Cain was obligated to tell Roemer only what he knew about others, but the confidentiality agreement shielded Roemer from accessing any guilty knowledge on the part of Cain's illegal activities.

Roemer pulled the same kind of stunt for which John Connolly in Boston had been prosecuted in 2000. Connolly protected his informant Billy "Whitey" Bulger while Bulger killed off the Boston Italian Mafia. The only difference between Connolly and Roemer is that Roemer never got caught.

Roemer is an absolute liar, when he claims in his book not to know anything about the assassination conspiracy. Roemer did know there was an assassination plot to kill Kennedy because I had told him of such a scheme in 1962 involving the CIA, Roselli, Giancana and Cain.

Roemer's answer to me was, "Your source is crazy."

Of course, Cain was not about to tell Roemer anything concerning Giancana, or the CIA plot to kill Castro or Kennedy.

Cain knew that Roemer could have turned on Cain in a heart beat and could have had criminal charges brought against Cain at any moment.

Although Cain had been a cop for about ten years, he and Giancana hit it off well. Cain was good looking and smart as a whip. Cain had an IQ of 145. He was a genius in mathematics and he spoke five languages fluently. He was a top marksman having been trained by the Chicago Police Department. When Giancana offered his protégé, Richard Cain, to the CIA, they accepted him with open arms and Cain became a full-blown CIA asset.

Roemer writes that Cain and Giancana were also good buddies whooping it up in various foreign countries. Cain did a 'sweep' of Sam's various offices in Chicago looking for FBI bugs. Now if Cain and Giancana thought the FBI was bugging their various places, they certainly would not talk about killing Kennedy. But, Bill Roemer was naive enough to think that because he didn't hear a single word over any of the FBI's listening devices about their involvement in the Kennedy assassination that Giancana and Cain were not culpable in a conspiracy to kill Kennedy.

Roemer was surprised when Cain told him in 1971 that Giancana had an interest in cruise ships. Now, one would think that Giancana would talk about his interest in cruise ships over a bug. If Roemer did not hear about Giancana's cruise ship investments over a bug, Roemer certainly would not hear about the JFK assassination over a bug, especially when Roemer did not speak Italian or Spanish.

Cain was smart enough not to divulge that he may have found Mo and other bugs planted by the FBI just so that Cain could find out from Roemer exactly how much the FBI knew and when they knew it.

It is interesting to note that Roemer made a movie with Sam Giancana's daughter, Antoinette. What is even more amazing is that Roemer writes in the introduction to his book on Tony Accardo, FBI# 1410106, that, "I hold the memory of Tony Accardo higher than I do the memory of her (Antoinette's) father (Sam Giancana.)"

Roemer writes that Accardo "was guilty of the most heinous crimes..." Bill continues that, "I cannot let my respect for the man overcome impartiality."

I find it difficult to accept Bill Roemer's many laudatory comments about Chicago's various underworld characters. Roemer does not write in any of his books about his having put the bad guys in jail. It is always some other agent that seemed to get a conviction for a Chicago gangster. Why is that?

On December 20, 1973, a masked gunman approached Richard Cain in Rose's Sandwich Shop and blasted Cain point-blank in the face with a shotgun in the typical Chicago gangland style. It was speculated that Marshall Caifano had learned of Cain's honorary status as a Special Agent of the FBI, which had been given to Cain by Bill Roemer. It has been presumed that Caifano received permission from mob boss Tony Accardo, whom Roemer so dearly admired, to whack Cain. Caifano's wife, Darlene, had been interviewed by Ralph Hill in my North Lake Shore Drive apartment several times in 1961-62.

It is unbelievable that Roemer did not protect his best informant when the going got tough. Tony Accardo allegedly gave the nod to whack Cain and yet Roemer writes a book in honor of the Mafia boss. I don't get it.

Ralph Hill told me that Bill Roemer broke down and cried when Cain was murdered. If Bill Roemer cried when Cain died then there is no way Roemer would admit to the world that Cain was involved in the JFK assassination.

In 2004, a reliable source, who was acquainted with Mrs. Richard Cain, advised me that Mrs. Cain told the source in a privileged communication that Richard Cain was on the Grassy Knoll at the time Kennedy was assassinated and that Cain was dressed in a dark suit and tie. Cain reportedly was not wearing a police uniform the day JFK was killed. Cain was, however, wearing his usual horn-rimmed glasses. The source also said that after the shooting at Dealey Plaza, Cain went around telling everyone that "everything is under control." This source has requested anonymity for fear of being killed.

A second source also advised me in 2004 that she had heard from sources close to Mrs. Richard Cain that Richard Cain was on the Grassy Knoll when President Kennedy was killed. This second source was acquainted with a relative of Chicago's Mob Boss Tony "Batters" Accardo. Tony Accardo was given the nickname "Joe Batters" by Al Capone after Accardo killed one of Capone's rivals with a baseball bat. This second source also requested anonymity for fear of being killed.

Both sources reported that after Richard Cain was killed gangland style in Chicago in 1973, Mrs. Cain moved to Florida and was reportedly receiving a monthly income from an unknown source.

Richard Cain was murdered at age 42.

Sam Giancana was shot to death in 1975 and Johnny Roselli was butchered in 1976.

CHAPTER 9
Judy Campbell Exner a Kennedy Lover

J udith Campbell Exner was born Judith Katherine Inmoor on January 11, 1934 to a German family in New York. She later moved to Los Angeles and married actor William Campbell in 1952. She was divorced in 1959.

While in Hollywood she met Frank Sinatra who introduced Judy to Senator John F. Kennedy. Campbell and Kennedy struck up an affair which continued into his presidency. Her affair with Jack was just one of Hoover's mouth watering nuggets used to muscle the President.

Frank Sinatra also introduced Campbell to Sam Giancana, the Chicago mob boss. This piqued the interest of the FBI agents working on the THP squad in Chicago. Ralph Hill was especially interested in talking to Judy Campbell because Giancana was assigned to Hill. Roemer could not believe that President Kennedy would sleep with the same woman that Sam Giancana was having as a live-in guest. Roemer was a golden boy and so he could not think ill of anyone, including Mob bosses and Mafia hit men.

I was in the process of getting a divorce during this time and so I rented a small apartment on the 29ᵗʰ floor of a building on Chicago's North Lake Shore Drive overlooking Lake Michigan and what was then called the Outer Drive.

One day Hill asked if he could use my apartment for an interview. I thought nothing of it. Hill was working in the area where Giancana had some of his businesses and so I said yes to Hill. I had an extra set of keys to the front door and to the apartment. I told Hill that when he is done interviewing just give me a call at the office. If Hill had an extended interview, or if he was running late, he would send me a message and I would go to dinner at Jim Saine's Restaurant on Rush Street, which was about a five minute walk from the apartment.

Ralph Hill and Maz Rutland both were using my apartment for interviews. One day Hill asked me, with a grin of the Cheshire cat on his face, "Guess who I interviewed in your apartment yesterday?"

I asked, "I don't have the slightest idea. Maybe Sam Giancana?" I was joking.

Ralph chuckled and said, "Not Sam. His girl friend Judy Campbell."

I was working Cuban counterintelligence and had no knowledge of the names of folks in the Mafia. I asked, "Who the hell is Judy Campbell?"

"Are you joking?"

"No, I'm not joking. Who the hell is Judy Campbell?"

"Sam Giancana is balling Judy along with Frank Sinatra and President Kennedy."

"Honest to God, Ralph. You're going to get me killed, or at least fired, or both."

"Don't sweat it, Swearingen. No one will ever know about your apartment."

"What if Hoover finds out. He will fire my ass."

"Hoover already knows about Judy."

"What?" I shouted.

"Hoover wants all the info I can get on Judy because she is shacking up with JFK."

I looked at Hill for several minutes, then said, "Damn it Ralph, if Hoover doesn't fire both of us, Giancana will kill us both."

"Relax. No problem."

"That's easy for you to say. It's my apartment."

"No one knows but us."

"Well, Judy knows. How about Roemer?"

"I'm not telling Roemer squat."

"How about Maz?"

"Yeah, but he won't say anything."

"What are you going to tell Hoover?"

"I'm telling Hoover only what he wants to hear, that I interviewed Campbell about Giancana, Sinatra, and Kennedy and that she said she is screwing all three."

"I don't feel too well."

"Let's go have a drink. You'll feel better when I explain everything."

Ralph assured me that Giancana would never find out that he had used my apartment to interview Judy Campbell. I trusted Hill that he would never say a word to Hoover.

Ralph said, "Hoover wants the Campbell-Giancana info so that he can blackmail Kennedy."

"I hope you're right."

Chicago reported to Hoover that Campbell was sleeping with Frank Sinatra, Sam Giancana, and Kennedy. When Hoover heard this about Campbell, Hoover quickly had a meeting with President Kennedy and JFK's love affair with Campbell stopped immediately. However, Ralph continued to use my apartment for interviews.

Before Judy Campbell Exner died in 1999, she wrote a book about her affairs with Giancana and President Kennedy, which was published in 1977 and became a best seller. I have not read her book. Hill told me everything that I needed to know.

CHAPTER 10
Darlene Caifano a Mobster's Wife

Ralph Hill told me that Marshall Caifano was a Chicago mob made guy. Caifano was Chicago's guy on the West Coast and in Las Vegas. According to rumors, Caifano had followed in Johnny Roselli's footsteps.

It was a shock when Hill told me about his interview with Judy Campbell in my apartment on North Lake Shore Drive, so when he told me about Darlene Caifano's interview it was not that much of a surprise. It was vintage Hill, but I was still worried.

Hill told me that Darlene was a Kentucky hillbilly. Even though she had been in my apartment a few times Hill assured me there was no problem because Sam Giancana was having an affair with Darlene. Wow! Now that grabbed my attention. All I needed was to have my apartment caught up in a love triangle between the FBI, Caifano, and Giancana. I figured, "What the hell, I may as well die young and have a good looking corpse."

I asked Hill, "Does Roemer know about Darlene?"

"He knows about Darlene, but I have not told him where I am holding my interviews."

"Does Caifano know about my apartment?

Hill answered. "Not unless Darlene told him, and I don't think she will. Caifano might go ape shit if he knew Darlene was shacking up with the FBI."

"Oh, swell."

Hill replied, "I interviewed Caifano and told him that Sam Giancana was sleeping with Darlene. Caifano was flattered as hell that Sam liked his wife."

"I thought mafia guys respected other guy's wives?"

"That is only Hollywood movie bullshit."

"Oh shit, Ralph. I hope you are wearing condoms."

Both Hill and Rutland used my apartment for interviews. The place was clean when they left and they always donated a bottle of Cutty Sark Scotch whisky on the bar counter. They usually returned my apartment key in an envelope in my mail folder. My apartment was my contribution to fighting the Chicago mob.

CHAPTER 11
To Kill a President

Chicago, 1962

It was another typically hot day in the inner city of Chicago and so I drove the bureau car out to the Adler Planetarium and Astronomy Museum overlooking Grant Park and Grant Harbor, where it was usually a little cooler near Lake Michigan. Hoover's FBI did not provide air-conditioned cars to field agents in those days. I was not about to spend the afternoon, on the West Side of town, in a hot car, listening to Ramon talk about how he had survived the Bay of Pigs invasion and how bad Cuba is under the dictatorship of Fidel Castro. The heat did not bother Ramon because he grew up in Cuba and so it didn't matter to Ramon where we talked. I carried a new 8 by10 pad of note paper just in case Ramon had some funny jokes to tell.

I punched the cigarette lighter on the dash board. When it popped out I put the lighter to a Marlboro cigarette and puffed while glancing at the boats in Grant Harbor. I was thinking about being on my 25-foot sailboat, which was tied to one of the moorings. I wondered why Ramon had asked to see me again after the way I had treated him in 1960 when he laid out the plans for the Bay of Pigs invasion, which I had thought was total and complete lunacy.

Ramon was not expecting me to apologize, but I said, "I'm sorry Ramon, for not believing you about the Bay of Pigs."

Ramon said, "That's okay, Señor Swearingen. I understand that you love your country very much and that you have the highest respect for the CIA, but now there are a few bad apples in the CIA that are planning to kill President Kennedy."

I nearly choked on the cigarette smoke. "Damn it, Ramon! Can't you wait until I exhale before saying something like that?" Horrified, I asked, thinking it was a clear and present danger. "Do you know when or where?"

"Not exactly. The Chicago Mafia wants to do it in Chicago, but Kennedy has no plans to travel to Chicago soon."

"Then where?"

"The shooting will take place somewhere outside of Washington, D.C., where the Mafia has better control. It definitely will not be in Washington, D.C. Trafficante wants to do it in Florida."

"How do you know this?"

"I have connections in Miami and I spend a lot of time in Florida. I trained at the CIA camp in Florida before the Bay of Pigs invasion. Remember, I told you all about the Bay of Pigs and you kicked my ass out of the car? I know thousands of Cubans, in and out of Cuba. You name somebody and I have probably met him."

"You're funny. I hardly know anybody of importance from Cuba. Do you know anyone from Chicago?"

"I have not met the man, but he is called Sam Gold. He is actually Sam Giancana, Chicago's top boss. The CIA trained Sam Gold how to kill Fidel Castro at the JM/Wave camp in Florida."

"Ramon, if this guy you are talking about actually is Sam Giancana, he doesn't need to be taught how to kill anybody. He has been whacking thugs since he was a kid. Giancana started working for Al Capone during the 1930s prohibition."

Ramon was beginning to sound a little nutty again. I asked, "Who else is in on this crazy caper?"

Ramon said, "A loud mouth by the name of Johnny Roselli."

Johnny Roselli had been in the newspapers, but I wanted to see what Ramon knew, so I asked, "What do you know about him?"

"Roselli is the Chicago mob representative in Las Vegas. He supposedly works for Sam."

Ramon seemed to know what he was talking about because Roselli was actually the tie in between Howard Hughes and the Mafia from Chicago, Miami, and New Orleans, according to Roemer and Hill. "Do you know anyone else?"

"Si. Louis Santos from Miami. Now this guy is a real big shot. He used to be big in Cuba when Batista was there. The CIA referred to him as Louis Santos when we were at the camp, but I was told by Cuban friends in Miami that he is actually Santo Trafficante, the Miami Mafia boss."

"Ramon, I think you are traveling in some pretty big company, or you are one hell of a story teller."

"No, senor. I'm not pulling your chain. All these big shot gangsters were in Cuba when Batista was there. They are the ones who ran the gambling casinos. They brought tourists to Cuba. They are our friends."

"Okay, continue. I have lots of time and lots of note paper."

"There is Carlos from New Orleans."

"Who is Carlos?"

"I have been told that Carlos is Carlos Marcello. His real name is Calogero Minacore. He is the big boss in New Orleans."

"Yeah, I've heard the name Marcello from my friends in the office. I have not heard the name Minacore."

CHAPTER 12
"Indio"

Ramon flashed a big smile like he was telling me something I wanted to hear. Actually, if what Ramon was saying was true, I didn't want to hear about these big Mafia bosses from around the country talking about killing Kennedy. I was extremely uncomfortable.

Ramon asked, "Have you heard of the Indian, Sanchez?"

"How would I know anyone from India?"

"No, he is not from India. Sanchez is an American Indian. He works for the CIA. We call him 'Indio' for short."

(It should be noted that the New Orleans District Attorney Jim Garrison had received an anonymous letter claiming that a person named 'Indio' was a member of the hit team at Dealey Plaza when President Kennedy was assassinated. Jim Garrison never made the connection).

I took another drag on the cigarette. I didn't know whether to kick Ramon out of the car or go hide in a box somewhere. "Where did you meet this guy Indio?"

"He trained us at JM/Wave in Florida."

"Really? I suppose you're going to tell me Indio is employed by the CIA?"

"Yep, how'd you guess? He works out of Langley, Virginia. His real name is David Sanchez. He is a real government employee."

"You seem to know more about the Mafia and the CIA than the FBI does."

"Remember these guys were our friends in Cuba and the CIA has become our friends because the CIA wants to get back into Cuba. It really is easy to understand."

"So, what is the plan?"

"Different cities that Kennedy may travel to are setting up groups. Each group will recruit a political jerk that is crazy enough to take a shot at the President. The different teams will make sure that Kennedy is killed, without it looking like a Mafia hit, that's where the CIA comes in, and then the patsy, who takes the first shot, will be flown out of the country. If something goes wrong, the patsy will be killed. It is a very simple plan. The idea is to make it look like there was just one assassin. We practiced this in Florida when Castro was the target. The problem was that we couldn't get close to Castro because his security knows who we are. Shooting Kennedy will be much easier than shooting Castro."

"But, why are you telling me all of this?"

"Because I don't want to see Kennedy killed. He is basically a good man. Kennedy is not the Cuban problem. Castro is the problem. I don't think Kennedy should be killed just because he didn't back the Bay of Pigs. Many of my friends do not agree with me. That is why I am telling you. Maybe you can do something to stop this madness."

Ramon was making sense, but I had no idea of how to stop the CIA. I said, "I have no idea how to go about preventing the CIA from killing someone. They are experts in the killing field. They are strange, to say the least."

CHAPTER 13
A Chicago Cop

In 1962, I began to worry about Ramon's safety because he was telling me something I did not want to hear. My own safety became a point of concern.

Somehow, Ramon knew, in 1962, that the Chicago Mafia and Cuban exiles were being trained by the CIA to kill President Kennedy.

The thought that a foreigner was telling me that the President of the United States was going to be assassinated by the CIA, the Mafia, and Cuban exiles was beyond belief. The thought was awesome.

I asked, "Is there anyone else?"

Ramon replied, "Si, a bad Chicago cop."

"What?" I exclaimed. This conspiracy plot was becoming stranger by the minute. Now Ramon was adding the Chicago cops?

"Well, not really a cop. He was caught and forced to resign."

Now very curious, I asked, "What's his name? What did he do?"

"His name is Richard Cain. He is also called the Professor."

"What did he do?"

"Cain used to collect the mob's payoff money and distribute it to the different officers on the take."

"So why did Cain get fired?"

"Well, he roughed up a gay guy and the man died, so the police had to fire Cain to save face."

"Did you ever meet this guy Cain?"

"No, I didn't actually meet him face to face, but I have seen him and I have heard a lot about him. He is a real sharp guy, very intelligent, but he can be a real bad dude when he wants to be. That is why he was recruited for the Florida training. He speaks Spanish as well as my Cuban friends."

"Would Cain get involved in trying to kill Kennedy?"

Ramon glanced at the planetarium and then looked back at me. "It is hard to say. Sam Giancana thinks Cain is great. If Giancana needed help he would pick Cain because he is a known and trusted quantity."

I had taken so many notes that I was running out of paper.

I didn't know whether Ramon was for real or whether he had made up this story from reading the Miami newspapers because there was not any of this kind of nonsense in the Chicago newspapers. I played along because the FBI knew next to nothing about the Italian Mafia and absolutely nothing about the CIA. I knew enough to know that what the CIA was doing in Florida, if true, was illegal. If the information were true, then I was sitting on a time bomb with a very short fuse.

CHAPTER 14
Manuel Artime

I continued to ask Ramon about the CIA's plans, but he could not be more specific. He mentioned about two-dozen Spanish names that I no longer remember. They belonged to some group with a weird name. It was something sixty-six. Ramon could have been referring to a group that is now known as Alpha 66. He said he was getting his information from one of the leaders of the Cuban exiles in Florida by the name of Manuel Artime. The name was so different that my mental translation to English came out something like "Our Time." Would you spell his name, please?"

"A—ere—te—i- eme—e. Artime. Manuel Artime."

Ramon also said the CIA had trained Artime for the landing at the Bay of Pigs.

Ramon had mentioned many new sounding names, which were different from the names I had been used to from Puerto Rico such as Jimenez, Morales, Rodriguez and Gonzales. One time a different Puerto Rican informant had trouble with the Potomac River near Washington. He had pronounced it *Poe-toe-mawk*. After a few seconds I said, "Oh, you mean *PAH-toe-mick*." We both laughed, but it was a good lesson about languages that I never forgot.

I asked, "Ramon, why are you telling me all of this? If it is true, your life could be in danger. If it isn't true you are wasting my time."

Ramon said, "Manuel Artime was born in Cuba in 1932. He had supported Castro for a short period and then became an outspoken anti-Communist. Artime moved to the United States and joined up with Carlos Prio and Tony Verano to form a rebellion against Cuba. In 1960, Artime met Senator John F. Kennedy at the Democratic National Convention. Artime also knows Frank Sturgis, a pilot for the CIA."

I asked, "Are you getting your information from Artime?"

Ramon smiled and avoided my question. "I lost hundreds of friends at the Bay of Pigs when they landed on the beach along with Manuel Artime. It is the CIA's fault that they were killed or captured. I don't trust anyone else. If I talk to the wrong person, I am a dead man."

"What makes you think you can trust me?"

"I have many good friends in Chicago. They have said you are a good man and that you can be trusted."

Ramon may have been referring to the conflict I had with one of Fidel Castro's hit men who had come to Chicago to assassinate some of the outspoken anti-Castro Cuban exiles. It is quite possible that Castro's assassin was out to get Ramon.

A different informant had told me that Raul (a fictitious name, but a real person) had arrived in Chicago to kill certain Cubans at Fidel Castro's direction.

Mike Simon and I had confronted Castro's hit man, Raul, one evening on the street outside where Raul was staying. He flat out refused to cooperate. He was belligerent and hostile. Raul called us nearly all of the standard three to seven letter obscenities, plus a few I had never heard.

I was on the edge of losing control of myself with this arrogant bastard who had come to my country to kill Cuban exiles who had fled Castro's brutal dictatorship.

I said, "Okay, smart ass. If you aren't on the next plane back to Cuba, we are going to spread the word that you are an informant for the CIA and the FBI."

If looks could kill I would have dropped dead right then and there, on the sidewalk. Raul stepped forward and was so close to my face that I could smell his greasy taco breath. He shouted as his spit hit my face, "You *pendejo!*" He turned and ran to his car and then drove away.

The next day the informant called and asked, "What the hell did you say to Raul?"

I asked, "Why?"

The informant said, "His face was as white as a sheet and he was shaking like he had epilepsy. He left Chicago this morning on the first plane to Miami, on his way to Cuba."

I said to the informant, "I told Raul that if he didn't leave on the next plane for Cuba that I was going to spread the word that he was working for the CIA and the FBI."

The informant laughed. "I can't believe it. Castro's big tough guy was scared shitless."

I asked, "By the way, what does *pendejo* mean?"

"It means pubic hair. It is the lowest form of life a Cuban can call someone."

I was rather proud of getting one of Castro's assassins out of the country without firing a shot, or slapping him with a set of handcuffs, or creating a national incident, which could have ended up on the evening news. If I had embarrassed Hoover, he would have had me for lunch.

CHAPTER 15
Bill Harvey, the ZR/Rifle and Bannister

R amon continued with his impressive story about the CIA planning to kill the president.

I asked once more, "Can you think of anyone else from the CIA who is in on this?"

"Bill Harvey."

"Who is Bill Harvey?"

"Harvey is another CIA agent who trained us in Florida. I think he used to be FBI and Hoover fired him for some rules infraction. Harvey headed up the ZR/RIFLE team to kill Castro. He is another bad dude."

Ramon was right on the money again. Harvey had been transferred in 1947 for not maintaining regular contact with the office, one of Hoover's major rules for a field agent. We were told about Harvey in training school to make it clear that Hoover was serious about maintaining contact with the office. Bill Harvey, instead of accepting a transfer, had resigned from the FBI. Harvey could not be bothered with nitpicking rules such as letting Hoover know where Harvey was every hour of the day.

I asked Ramon, "What do you know about him?"

"Not much. I was told he worked with Sam Gold and Roselli on how to use a special rifle."

"What does he look like?"

"He's big, red faced, heavy set. He drinks a lot. He hates both of the Kennedy's."

"How old is he?"

"He's in his forties."

Ramon added, "The CIA, the Mafia and the Cubans are all mad at Kennedy for not supporting the invasion at the Bay of Pigs. Some guys are more pissed off than others. I think some of the rogue CIA agents are banding together with the Mafia to hit Kennedy fairly soon. The Chicago Mafia is especially mad because they put John Kennedy in the White House and now Bobby is trying to put them in jail. Sam Giancana and the other Mafia bosses are mad as hell at the Kennedy's because the Mafia wanted to get back their gambling casinos in Cuba. Kennedy refused to support the Bay of Pigs invasion at the last minute. It was a disaster."

I asked, "Do you know of anyone else remotely connected to this conspiracy?"

Ramon thought for a minute and then answered, "Guy Bannister is working with a potential patsy who works for the Fair Play for Cuba Committee. I don't know his name. From what I have heard about the patsy he is a real nut case."

(It is noted that many sources, including the Internet, spell Bannister with one n as Banister).

In 1954, there was a former SAC of Chicago named Guy Bannister, aka Banister. When Bannister introduced himself to the agents in Chicago he said, "If you have to use your weapon to subdue a subject, I want you to kill him. I don't want any agent telling me he shot someone in the foot or leg to cripple him." Bannister looked around the room at the expressions on agent's faces, including mine. I was shocked. Bannister continued, "If an agent has to kill a bank robber, the agent can come back to the office, put his feet up on my desk and dictate a memo to Hoover telling why he shot the man. This is not the Bureau policy, this is the Bannister policy."

There was a low rustle of whispers among agents.

One other time Guy Bannister replied to one of Hoover's questionnaires to the field, which were always answered with what Hoover wanted to hear. This time Bannister wrote to Hoover and said, "The Bureau has divorced itself from the field many years ago and has been living in a state of adultery ever since."

There was a big brouhaha in the agents' room when the rumor spread about Bannister's letter to Hoover. By return phone call, Johnny Mohr, Assistant Director in Charge of the Administrative Division, told Bannister that he, Bannister, was going to be transferred to Hawaii. Bannister reportedly said to Mohr, "The hell I am, I'm retiring."

Having worked for Bannister and knowing his right wing policies, I was not surprised to hear Ramon mention Bannister's name. Someone in New Orleans, who was close to Lee Harvey Oswald, was furnishing information about the Fair Play for Cuba Committee. It turned out to be Guy Bannister the former SAC of the Chicago FBI office.

From what Ramon said, it was quite obvious that President John F. Kennedy had accomplished exactly what Fidel Castro had done. JFK had pissed off the CIA, the Mafia and the Cuban exiles all in one poor executive decision when he reneged, at the last moment, and did not support the Bay of Pigs invasion.

Did President John F. Kennedy actually expect the Bay of Pigs fiasco to just go away after he broke his promise to support the CIA, the Mafia and the Cubans?

Knowing what Ramon had told me, I could see the assassination coming a year before it happened, but my superiors did not believe the CIA could carry out such a dastardly deed as to kill the President of the United States.

CHAPTER 16
Supervisor Culkin and the CIA

In mid-October, 1962, Ramon phoned me and said that a tentative plan had been worked out with Giancana, Roselli, Cain, Ruby, Ferrie, Bannister, and a patsy from New Orleans.

"Can you be more specific?"

"Yes, but not over the phone."

"Can we meet somewhere?"

"No. I'm leaving for Miami tomorrow for about a month. I'll call you when I get back in December. I should know more when I get back from Miami. I'll be seeing Artime. There is no hurry, as I understand the schedule."

"Okay, Ramon. Have a safe trip. Maybe we can get together before Christmas?"

"Sounds good. Happy Holidays."

I did not know for sure what Ramon meant by "tentative plan," but I assumed it had to do with the mob, the Cubans, and the CIA's plan to kill Kennedy. I had no idea what I could do to thwart any action against the President when Ramon returned from Miami. I crossed my fingers and hoped that day would never come.

I told Bill Roemer what Ramon had said but he was not interested. He thought Ramon was a nut case. I decided to tell Culkin and then write an office memo to the SAC under the caption "Chicago Mob and the CIA Plan to assassinate President Kennedy." Miscellaneous File 62-0.

There was no one in Supervisor Joseph Culkin's office except Joe himself. He appeared to be proof reading a report. I walked into the all-glass enclosure, which was about ten feet by ten feet, and sat down.

Joe looked up and made his usual greeting, "How ya hittin'em?"

I laughed and said, "Out in center field." Joe normally wasn't expecting a response, but I was trying to be funny. I began to lay out what Ramon had said including the names, which Culkin had heard me mention in other conversations. Culkin was upset with my continued reference to the CIA and the Chicago mob planning to kill Kennedy. It sounded nuts, even to me, but my job was to report what sources told me, not to make a judgmental call as to its validity.

Culkin usually took a drag on his cigarette and then exhaled through his nostrils like a cartoon dragon when he was perturbed. "Is that your joke for the day, Ivan?" he asked, as smoke came out his nose.

I had earned the nickname Ivan when Culkin and I worked surveillances together when I dressed up like a Russian to keep warm during Chicago's cold winters with the wind whipping off Lake Michigan.

"It's no joke. My source is serious."

"What does Roemer think?"

"He thinks its bullshit."

"So do I."

I replied, "I'm going to write it up just to cover my ass. Sixty-two Zero. You can do whatever you want with it."

"Don't bother me with crap like that. The CIA would

never kill the President. Remember that garbage Jose gave to you about the NPPR planning to kill Hoover?"

"Yes, but they had already shot up Congress. What was I supposed to do, just forget it?"

"I had to explain to Inspector James B. Adams why your overtime was running over five hours a day. More than double the office average."

"So what is a little overtime if it is going to save the Director's life?"

"But you are saying the CIA is planning to kill the President. Do you know how crazy that sounds?"

"So it sounds crazy. It is not my job to judge the information I receive."

"You are sounding crazy because you can't judge what is real and what is fiction."

"Well, let the CIA prove they are not making plans with the Chicago mob to kill Kennedy. Let Hoover make it public in the media and then it will never happen."

"You have a point, but that will never happen."

"Okay. Have it your way. I'm dictating a memo."

"Whatever."

I dictated a memo to the 62-0 file stating briefly what Ramon had said about the CIA plotting with the Chicago Mafia and the Cuban exiles to kill President Kennedy. I wrote in the memo that I had discussed the subject with Roemer, Hill, and Rutland of the THP squad and that they all thought it was nonsense.

I remarried on November 21, 1962. Hoover suddenly transferred me to Louisville, Kentucky, where I reported for duty on January 7, 1963.

I left Chicago without having a chance to talk to Ramon

again about what additional information he may have received when he visited Miami in October and November of 1962.

I originally thought Hoover transferred me because my new wife had supported Henry Wallace for President after Wallace had been vice-president under Harry Truman, or so this is what Culkin wanted me to believe. The FBI supposedly considered Paula, my new wife, a security risk. However, the FBI conducted a full field investigation into Paula's background, including her relatives, and she was found _not_ to be a security risk. Why then was I transferred shortly after I had insisted that a Cuban exile was telling the truth that the CIA was conspiring with the Chicago Mob and Cuban exiles to kill President Kennedy?

Culkin suggested that I tell the other agents on the squad that Louisville was an old Office of Preference (OP) that I had forgotten about. This was not true and I had told Culkin as much.

Ninety days after being transferred to Louisville, I was again transferred to the remote area of Paintsville, Kentucky. This time it was to a former two man resident agency (RA) where the two agents had been transferred to other assignments. I was the sole RA and I had no other agents to talk to about the CIA's plan to kill Kennedy. I was now doing the work of two agents. Paintsville had always been a two-man RA, which covered five counties. I remained in Paintsville for two years. I was then transferred to London, Kentucky, another two-man RA. The two agents at London were transferred out and I was again alone. Two agents were transferred to Paintsville to replace me. I remained in London until 1968 when I was transferred to New York City. Two men were transferred to London to replace me when I went to New York City. I had been in two different RAs for five years all by myself doing the work of two agents at each RA.

If my wife Paula was supposedly a security risk why then was I transferred to New York City the spy capital of the world?

CHAPTER 17
Friday, November 22, 1963

Washington, D.C.
It was another day that will live in infamy
To many others it was the end of Camelot.

I t was the last day of a two week In-Service training session at the FBI National Academy located on the U.S. Marine Corps Base at Quantico, Virginia. The air was invigorating when I went for a two-mile dawn run. By 10:00 a.m. it had warmed up and it was comfortable in our regimented suit and tie. The forty white FBI agents boarded the old gray school bus, driven by a black man, for our trip back to Washington, D.C.

The FBI did not have black agents, or other minorities in 1963, but it did have black janitors and chauffeurs. One black janitor in the Chicago FBI office, with a high school education, had been anointed as a token black Special Agent in 1954 when J. Edgar Hoover was accused of racial discrimination.

We had just completed two weeks of In-service training, to hone our investigative skills and to sharpen our ability with various firearms. The FBI National Academy has the relaxed ambience of a small university set between tall pines and colorful deciduous trees. Smooth blacktop roads wander through the well-groomed blue grass grounds. Marines were often seen marching on the roads past the FBI Academy. They frequently shouted in cadence the letters L-A-V-A, which was for the Lava soap sponsor of the ABC TV series "The FBI" with Ephrem Zimbalist, Jr. where Zimbalist was an FBI Inspector and quick on the draw.

The bus driver delivered us to the Department of Justice building on Pennsylvania Avenue, between Ninth and Tenth Streets, in Washington, D.C., where the FBI had its Bureau headquarters. We dropped our luggage in one of the classrooms and went to lunch. Little did we know that this particular day would be a day of infamy and a turning point in history... especially for the FBI!

The offices of FBI Director J. Edgar Hoover, the Omniscient One, were on the floor above the classrooms and away from the hustle and bustle of the brick agents. Hoover made certain that the FBI functioned to his liking, controlling press releases and the phony statistics that annually dazzled Congress. Hoover did not associate with what he considered his private army of all men. He was isolated in his own ivory tower. He used a private elevator to get from his chauffeur driven black, bullet proof Cadillac limousine to his private office. One day a young clerk was caught using Hoover's elevator and the clerk was fired on the spot.

It was 2:10 p.m. We had just returned from a leisurely lunch, the first such chance we had to relax in the past two weeks. This was the final hour of lectures before leaving for our respective offices of assignment. A few of the agents were struggling to stay awake. I checked my airline schedule and the tickets. I was anxious to get back to Louisville where my wife, Paula, and I had planned to celebrate our first wedding anniversary.

Suddenly, the front door of the classroom flew open. Inspector W. Mark Felt, from the Training and Inspection Division, ran in and yelled, "President Kennedy has just been shot in Dallas! We don't have any details. You're being released immediately to make connections back home."

As Inspector Felt, who is now known as 'Deep Throat' from the Watergate scandal, hurried out the front door, I went out the back door to meet him. Since my name started with an S, I always sat in the last row of any class, close to the back door. I walked up to Felt and said, "My bags are all packed and ready to go, sir. I'd like to volunteer for the Kennedy special. All I have to do is get the next flight to Dallas."

Mark Felt said, and I will never forget his words, "You have been away from home for two weeks. We'll get some other agents to go to Dallas on Monday."

"But, sir, I have reason to believe Kennedy's shooting may involve a conspiracy between the CIA, the Mafia and some Cuban exiles. I can be there in a few hours. If you pick other agents from around the country they will have to dictate leads on their cases, go home, pack, make reservations, say goodbye to their kids, and then fly to Dallas. This whole In-service class could be in Dallas before dinner this evening."

"That's okay. We'll handle it. You go home and take care of the work you've neglected for the past two weeks." The Inspector turned on his right heel and walked away.

CHAPTER 18
Go back to Paintsville

The President of the United States had just been shot to death and the only thing Mark Felt could think of was to send forty freshly trained and experienced agents back to their home offices and to send me back to my home office of Paintsville, Kentucky, to work some old dog eared cases consisting mostly of stolen cars that had been burned to a crisp and were not worth junk parts. Just because Hoover hated Kennedy, Mark Felt would drag his feet on this investigation. I knew then that the Kennedy assassination cover-up had started and that Mark Felt and James H. Gale would play a major part in the obfuscation of the truth.

(It is noted that Mark Felt was indicted in 1978, by a Federal Grand Jury in Washington, D.C., for violating the civil rights of members of the Weather Underground Organization (WUO), a group of radical college kids from wealthy families. Felt was convicted in 1980, but pardoned by President Ronald Reagan).

I had wanted to go to Dallas and begin to look for evidence indicating that Ramon had surely been wrong about the conspiracy to assassinate President Kennedy. Guilt had begun to haunt me. I didn't know what to do. In 1962, I had to be careful of saying anything about what I knew because J. Edgar Hoover would have fired me for incompetence. I had already been transferred to Paintsville, Kentucky, for reasons unknown to me. I had not received any letters of censure and Louisville had not been my "office of preference." My work performance in Chicago had been rated as excellent. My supervisor thought I had done an outstanding job in matters concerning the Nationalist Party of Puerto Rico (NPPR).

My work on Cuban counterintelligence against Premier Fidel Castro had been unparalleled. Hoover had sent me a letter stating that he was pleased with my Spanish language skills.

I did not know of any rational explanation for an agent, such as myself, who had more than ten years experience in the foreign counterintelligence field and who had performed in an excellent fashion, to have been transferred to a one-man resident agency in eastern Kentucky that covered five counties where my job was to arrest military deserters, locate men who were delinquent with their Draft Board, recruit clerical employees for FBI headquarters in Washington, D.C., investigate railroad bombings, chase hunters who had shot migrating birds, search for individuals who had purchased gasoline with a stolen credit card, and investigate stolen cars that were usually burned to a crisp.

CHAPTER 19
Flight to Louisville

Ramon had unloaded a tremendous confidence with my promise not to tell a soul. I knew that as soon as I had accepted his faith that I carried his burden and that I held his life in my hands. One Anti-Castro Cuban source had already been killed. The source had given me photos he had taken on the sly of some Soviet ships in Havana's harbor. With Hoover's permission I personally turned over the photos to the CIA in Chicago. I was not about to see another informant killed as a result of the CIA's bungling ways. I sensed that what Ramon had told me about the Mafia and the CIA, the last time I spoke to him, was true. Once before he had told me an outrageous story about the CIA and the Bay of Pigs, which I learned later had been true.

Paintsville was the epitome of the backwater boondocks—which can be described as an uninhabited area with thick natural vegetation, as some back woods or marsh. The population of Paintsville was 2,000, counting all the dogs, cats, and chickens. I was caught between a rock and a hard spot. If it ever came out that I knew about a CIA plan to kill the President I could end up six feet under.

I had stood outside the In-Service classroom absolutely dumbfounded as I watched Inspector Mark Felt disappear down the hall and around a corner. I returned to the classroom where the instructor had already dismissed the class.

I grabbed my suitcase and went down to the street to catch a cab to the airport. The cab driver tuned his radio to the constant news about the Kennedy assassination. Reports came over the air that a lone gunman had shot the President. Somehow I felt better knowing that I was out of a really tough spot and that the CIA and the Mob didn't do it. But if Ramon was correct then I had a real problem and I worried about whether the shooters were the CIA, the Chicago Mob, the Miami Mob, or the Cuban exiles, who also hated Kennedy for not supporting them at the Bay of Pigs.

The plane ride from Washington to Louisville filled me with doubt and confusion of what I should do or what I should have done as I thought of the President. Visions of John Kennedy playing with little John had touched me to the point of nearly crying. The thoughts of the President's children running to him as he descended from the helicopter, or as he played football on the White House lawn, or as little John crawled around in the oval office, haunted me. If what Ramon had said were true, how could I have stopped the Mafia and the CIA from assassinating President Kennedy? The flight to Louisville was filled with surrealism.

The plane arrived in Louisville just before dinner. Paula waited at the gate. She bubbled over with anticipation of my arrival. She had worn her yellow dress with a very short hemline. It thrilled me just to watch her walk toward me. Paula looked better than the day we were married. She had driven from Paintsville to greet me. I knew how much she hated the narrow, twisting road through the hills of Kentucky. She did not like the drive even when I drove our 1959 Cadillac. We hugged and kissed as though I had just arrived home from six months of sea duty. I appreciated her desire to meet me in

Louisville. I now felt as though everything was back to normal for me.

Paula asked, "Did you hear about Kennedy?"

"Yes," I replied. We didn't dwell on Kennedy because we were more interested in going out for a good steak dinner. Later we watched TV until it was time to go to sleep in our little motel room.

<u>November 22, 1963, had been an unreal day for everyone.</u>

CHAPTER 20
November 23, 1963

It was almost a Reprieve

On Saturday morning, November 23, 1963, I went out to the motel parking lot and discovered that the bulbous tail lights on our white 1959 Cadillac had been stolen. I reported the theft to the Louisville Police Department and then called GEICO insurance company. After breakfast I went to the FBI office.

About ten agents had been called to work. Louisville had rush leads on the Kennedy assassination. The standard routine, in a major case like this, was to check various sources such as live informants, police department files, and credit records, for any information concerning the subject, which in this case was Lee Harvey Oswald. We were looking for accomplices. All live informants had to be contacted immediately and alerted to report any information on Oswald or any of his friends and relatives. The major police departments in Kentucky had to be contacted for any record of Oswald, which could offer additional leads. Credit bureaus in major cities had to be checked on Monday when the offices opened for business. It may sound like a lot of detailed work for nothing, but this is what the FBI is good at and how we operated under J. Edgar Hoover. The FBI literally left no stone unturned. Nothing was left to chance. If there were any information in Kentucky about Lee Harvey Oswald, it was Louisville's job to dig it up immediately, not six months or a year later. The FBI did not want some smart aleck defense attorney to spring a surprise on the U. S. Attorney during a trial of such magnitude. The anticipated trial of Oswald was already being called the trial of the century.

The Louisville office was buzzing with tales about Lee Harvey Oswald. Any FBI office was the place to get the latest in rumors. It was better and faster than a news bureau. Joe Gamble, the assistant special agent in charge, (ASAC) seemed to be in charge of the investigation on Saturday because the SAC was out playing golf and could not be bothered. Gamble was also in charge of the rumor mill. Several of us were in the agent's bullpen area with Joe Gamble. I did not see the Special Agent in Charge (SAC).

I jokingly said to Joe Gamble, "Who is going to be the new SAC in Dallas."

Joe Gamble frowned and said, "What's the matter with you, Swearingen? Don't you have any respect?"

I said, "I heard Oswald was an FBI informant working for James Hosty." Joe Gamble glared at me. I didn't care what Gamble thought. I had been assigned to Paintsville, a one-man resident agency. It was the pits. Joe Gamble could not do a thing to me that would be worse than living in Paintsville.

A disciplinary transfer to any place in the country had to be a step up.

Some months earlier Gamble had jumped on me for not handling an old dog lead on time. I had been working in Johnson County one day when the Kentucky State Police relayed a message for me to call the Louisville office. It was hot and humid and I had been standing inside a telephone booth along a dusty road talking to Gamble about one case that had gotten very old. Joe Gamble was sitting in his air-conditioned office in Louisville. I said, "I'll cover the lead when I finish the more important work in my briefcase."

Gamble said, "How would you like a transfer to Jackson, Mississippi?"

"Good! I'll be ready at eight a.m. tomorrow!"

"You know I can't do that."

"You can if you want to."

"Just cover that lead before both of us get a letter of censure for delayed investigation."

"Okay, Joe. I'll do my best."

CHAPTER 21
Swearingen Has Balls

In 1970, I learned what Joe Gamble really thought of me. I had been assigned to the car squad in New York City, which also investigated bombing matters. I was then considered the FBI's terrorist bombing expert in 1969. Joe Gamble had been promoted to SAC of the FBI's New York City Security Division. Joe Gamble's security agents were looking for a Weatherman fugitive named Cathy Boudin, who had been seen running naked from the New York City townhouse that blew up on March 6, 1970. The explosion killed Weathermen Diana Oughton, Ted Gold, and Terry Robbins. Gamble requested that I lead raids on several New York City apartments in search of Cathy Boudin.

I asked Tommy Rogers, (a fictitious name to protect his identity) and one of the agents on the raiding party who worked for Gamble, "Why did Gamble want me? I'm not even in his division?"

Tommy replied, "Because Gamble said, 'Swearingen has balls.'"

During our search for Boudin we ran across one apartment dweller who did not want to open the door to the FBI. I shouted, "Open the God damned door before we blow it off the hinges." I motioned to the two agents carrying shotguns and shouted, "Okay guys, rack one in the chamber." The sound echoed in the hallway and was a formidable challenge to the person standing behind the closed door. Suddenly I heard the locks being unsnapped and dead bolts slammed open. I could hardly keep from laughing.

I stepped inside the apartment and exhibited my credentials to the small man by the door. I said, "I'm agent Swearingen of the FBI. We have an arrest warrant for Cathy Boudin."

He replied, "She isn't here."

I said, "Okay, we will look around to make sure you are telling the truth and then we will be on our way."

We searched the apartment but Boudin was nowhere in sight. The apartment dweller said, "I'm going to call my attorney and report your conduct."

I said, "Good. Here is my name." I pointed to my name in blue letters on the credentials. I said, "Make sure he spells it correctly. I don't like it when people misspell my name."

After we left the apartment, Tommy said, "Now I know why Gamble said you have balls. Were you actually going to blow the door off the hinges?"

"No, but that little twerp didn't know that I wouldn't."

CHAPTER 22
Oswald as an Informant

Director Hoover always transferred any SAC forthwith whenever a field office had a debacle of major proportions. And, if true, an FBI informant killing the President of the United States was an astronomical debacle.

I remembered the San Diego SAC, Ewell C. Richardson, who had been transferred in 1951 because a serial killer fled from the United States into Mexico through San Diego's territory. Mexico's Federal Police had apprehended the killer. Hoover had been embarrassed and so Hoover busted SAC Richardson to a brick agent and transferred him to Memphis, Tennessee. The San Diego SAC Richardson had interviewed me as an applicant for the position of a special agent, but he was my equal when I arrived in Memphis from training school just four months later. This is how Hoover treated his men. If something happened beyond their control, which embarrassed the egotistical pontifex, they were gone, out of sight.

I had expected Hoover to immediately replace SAC Gordon Shanklin in Dallas if the rumors were correct that Lee Harvey Oswald was the lone gunman and that he had been an FBI informant. That was enough for Hoover to transfer both the SAC and special agent James P Hosty, Jr. who reportedly handled Oswald. Hosty was in hot water up to his eyeballs. The Louisville office had already generated rumors that the FBI informant file on Oswald had been shredded. One rumor had it that Shanklin had ordered Hosty to flush the informant file down the toilet. This may or may not be true. There was so much confusion in Dallas at that time that no one could make sense of anything.

I telephoned a fellow agent that I knew in Dallas who had worked on the surveillance squad in Chicago.

"Hello, Joven. This is Wes Swearingen. How's your home on the range?"

We shot the bull for a few minutes then I asked, "Did you hear anything about the CIA and the Chicago mob being involved it killing Kennedy?"

Joven replied, "Yeah, but we have been ordered not to mention anything about a conspiracy. In fact, Hoover just laid down the law to Shanklin to make sure no one says anything to the press. Hoover said he would fire anyone who claims Oswald was an FBI informant or was not the lone assassin."

I asked, "Oh shit, what are you going to do?"

Joven replied, "I can't talk now. Call me back later. Shanklin is on the phone to Hoover every five minutes. I don't know who is going to have a baby first—Hoover or Shanklin."

"Okay Joven. I'll call you on Monday."

In all fairness to Agent James P. Hosty, Jr., who wrote a book entitled *ASSIGNMENT: OSWALD* and who reportedly had Oswald as an informant, I do not believe the rumors that were tossed about by the media and other sources in Dallas, including the rumors within the FBI. One source that gave Oswald an informant symbol number was so far off base that it is laughable beyond imagination.

However, it troubles me that FBI agent Will H. Griffin reportedly stated in public that Lee Harvey Oswald had been an FBI informant. The book *DEAD WITNESSES* lists Griffin as deceased in 1982 from cancer.

What does bother me immensely is the fact that Hoover, ADIC James Gale, and Inspector Mark Felt thought Oswald should have been on the Security Index (SI). Seventeen of Hoover's subordinates were censured as a result of Oswald not being on the SI. Whether or not Oswald qualified for the SI is beside the point. If Oswald was so important after the assassination then Oswald should have been interviewed by the FBI in New Orleans where he was publicly supporting Fidel Castro by passing out literature.

To my knowledge all Castro supporters were interviewed in Chicago. I know because I did many of the interviews myself. If Oswald had lived in Chicago he would have been interviewed. Why wasn't the FBI attempting to develop Oswald as an informant especially after Oswald attempted to kill Major General Edwin A. Walker on April 10, 1963 as Walker sat in his home in Dallas?

Someone is lying about Oswald, or the FBI completely dropped the ball. Gale and Felt should have brought Lee Harvey Oswald to the attention of Hoover so that Hoover could decide for himself what to do about Oswald. They obviously did not mention Oswald to Hoover.

According to what Ramon said, if Oswald was an informant then Oswald was working for the CIA, not the FBI. But, the FBI should have attempted to develop Oswald as an informant

CHAPTER 23
Louisville, November 25, 1963

On Monday, November 25, 1963, the Cadillac dealer replaced the taillights on my car. I spent the rest of the day reviewing files that needed priority attention when I got back to Paintsville. A stack of mail, which the Chief Clerk's office gave to me, was waiting for my attention.

It was not necessary to call Dallas on Monday. The earlier rumors that Fidel Castro was behind Kennedy's assassination had been discounted. Some rumors from good sources said that the CIA did it and that the Mafia was out for revenge.

One agent, whom I'll call Cadillac Jack, said, "The rumors that the CIA or the Mafia did this is crap, Wes. Lee Harvey Oswald is the only one who shot Kennedy."

"That's a relief."

"What did you say?"

"Oh! Nothing. It's a relief that the case is closed." Cadillac Jack knew little or nothing about the Chicago Mob and so I discounted much of what he said. Jack did not know that the CIA was backing Sam Giancana and Johnny Roselli in an effort to kill Fidel Castro. Jack's naiveté was understandable. Jack knew nothing about the CIA's training camp in Florida.

"Yeah, but we didn't have jurisdiction anyway. It is not a federal crime to kill a President."

"What? You mean a guy goes to jail if he shoots one of us,

but not if he shoots the President? I thought Congress would have made it a federal crime after Abraham Lincoln was shot."

"Hell, no. Congress would rather hound hippies who burn the flag than to jail a presidential assassin. Now that Jack Ruby shot Oswald, the state of Texas is handling this puppy. Of course with Oswald dead there is no case."

"I'll bet Hoover is as happy as a pig in mud?"

"You bet. Hoover hated Kennedy. Rumor has it that when Hoover told Clyde Tolson on Friday that the President was dead, Tolson just smiled and asked, 'Does this make your day Edgar, or what?'"

CHAPTER 24
Hoover declares Oswald as the lone assassin

Clyde Tolson had been Hoover's associate director and daily companion for forty years. They were inseparable. Agents had secretly speculated that they were lovers. There were rumors that Hoover had put Oswald up to shooting Kennedy. Now that rumor is malicious, baseless, and without merit. Although if Kennedy had tried to get rid of the FBI, the way it was rumored that Kennedy was trying to get rid of the CIA, there would have been a lot of FBI volunteers to neutralize Kennedy.

This country needs the FBI regardless of how incompetent it may seem at times or how often it covers up any wrongdoing.

I asked, "Then there's no cloak and dagger conspiracy?"

Jack replied, "Hell no. The only conspiracy is the cover-up."

"What do you mean?"

"Well, Hoover sent a memo to the White House saying that Oswald was the lone gunman."

"So?"

"Hoover isn't giving the White House all the facts."

"What else is there?"

"Edgar didn't tell the White House that we didn't tell Secret Service that we knew Oswald was potentially dangerous and that we had not included Oswald on the Security Index, like we should have."

"Uh-oh."

"The Bureau is going bananas. It's been suggested that we are partly responsible for Kennedy's assassination because we had not alerted Secret Service. Worse still, Dallas had that creep as an informant."

"Now what?"

"Hosty's butt is in a jam. After Jack Ruby shot Oswald at the Police Department, Shanklin gave Hosty some material and told him to deep six it."

"Did he?"

"Rumor has it that Hosty tore up a file on Oswald and flushed it down the toilet."

"Who is this guy Ruby? The name is familiar." Ramon had mentioned Jack Ruby, but I did not want to let on that I knew anything about a conspiracy. My ass would be in a vice if it went to the wrong people like Inspectors Mark Felt, or James Gale, who were looking for scapegoats at this point in time.

"Ruby is a former Chicago hood. He palled around with Mafia hit men."

By Monday the FBI clearly took the position that Lee Harvey Oswald was the lone killer. Hoover had not given an inch on the subject. Once the prophet had spoken, it was set in stone. It was rumored that Hoover did not want to anger the Mafia because it could expose Hoover and Clyde Tolson as long time lovers. As far as Hoover's FBI was concerned, the Kennedy assassination had been solved even though Kennedy had not yet been buried. It was what the FBI called "RUC." Referred Upon Completion to the office of origin. Hoover, Tolson, and their sycophant assistant directors wanted to return to the routine of reporting statistics on stolen cars recovered by the local police. The phony recovery statistics and phony fugitive apprehensions, that the FBI claimed, had been Hoover's bread and butter for nearly half a century. This is how Hoover got Congress to fund the ever growing bureaucracy.

FBI agents had an ongoing joke. When other agencies made a mistake, they apologized. When the FBI made a mistake, it just made another movie.

I was relieved that Hoover had closed the case on JFK. Ramon's information had thankfully appeared to be wrong although the fact that Jack Ruby had become involved bothered me. But, Oswald as the lone killer was a heavy load off my mind. No one could blame me for withholding information about Kennedy's assassination if a lone nut like Oswald had truly been the person responsible.

Top FBI officials such as ADIC James H. Gale, who had been the SAC of Chicago when I first learned of the plan to kill President Kennedy, Mark Felt and Hoover, did not understand the magnitude of the Bay of Pigs debacle. They thought that killing Kennedy was such an outrageous idea that they never confronted the CIA with what Ramon had reported.

Hoover prohibited all agents from saying anything publicly after Kennedy was killed. James Hosty, Jr. confirms this fact in his book.

WHAT MORE COULD I DO? I had written memos to the Miscellaneous 62-0 file and had told the "higher ups," including Gale when he was SAC in Chicago. I was ordered not to say anymore about Kennedy's assassination.

Hoover appointed ADIC James Gale to handle the grubby work of finding scapegoats just in case Hoover became embarrassed. I knew the CIA had orchestrated Kennedy's assassination and that rogue CIA agents were arranging to kill anyone who might talk. Individuals that Ramon told me about as being part of a conspiracy were dying in strange accidents, or were being murdered by persons unknown. I had to remain silent or I would have been just another "Dead Witness."

James Gale did as he was told. Oswald was found to be the lone assassin. In 1976, Gale testified before the United States House of Representatives Select Committee on Assassinations that as the ADIC he had disciplined 17 employees. This included the transfer of two supervisors out of Washington with a cut in salary. ADIC Bill Sullivan was also censured.

Gale testified that both he and Hoover thought Oswald should have been on the Security Index, but Gale never said a word to New Orleans or Dallas when he inspected those offices. Gale quickly added, after realizing that he said Oswald should have been on the Security Index, that if Oswald had been on the Security Index it would not have prevented the assassination.

Gale testified that he did not know whether the U.S. Secret Service would have been advised if Oswald had been on the security. Wow!

I am amazed and astounded that Gale, as the Chief Inspector, did not know that the Secret Service routinely received copies of FBI reports of individuals on the Security Index. Gale did not know the basic rules of the Security Index and he is claiming that Oswald should have been on the Security Index! Wow!

Gale did what he was told and Hoover's skirts remained as clean as a whistle.

CHAPTER 25
Later in Paintsville, Kentucky.

After returning to Paintsville, I waited for the dust to settle before calling my former partners and buddies. First I called Ralph Hill, my old drinking buddy from Chicago, who had been interviewing various Mafia girl friends in my apartment on North Lake Shore Drive in Chicago. Ralph had later been transferred to Miami and was the supervisor of the Top Hoodlum Program. Ralph Hill looked and acted a lot like the late actor Ralph Meeker when Meeker played Mike Hammer in the 1955 movie "Kiss Me Deadly," based on the best-selling book by Mickey Spillane. Ralph Hill fitted the Mike Hammer character perfectly. I used a pay phone so that I did not have to worry about any FBI switchboard operators or local telephone operators listening in on the conversation.

"Hey, Ralph, this is Wes Swearingen. How are you?"

"Where the hell are you, Wes?"

"I'm in Paintsville. I was attending the last day of In-service when Kennedy got shot."

"Are you still drinking Cutty Sark?"

"Absolutely. Are you still drinking gin martinis?"

"You know me, martinis every night."

"I switched to scotch because gin gives me a headache."

"Whatever turns you on."

"On my first day maneuvering these hairpin curves, I almost ran off a hundred-foot cliff. I had taken a 15-mph curve at 35."

"You're not on surveillance anymore. Slow down and enjoy the greenery."

"Hey! What's with this guy Jack Ruby?"

"He's a Chicago hood who runs Dallas for Sam Giancana. He used to pal around with Lenny Patrick and Davey Yaras who are two real bad-asses. They whacked James Ragen back in 1946 when he was the owner of the Continental Wire Service."

"Yeah, I remember you talking about a whack job on Ragen. Do you think the Outfit did Dallas?"

"They, the Cuban exiles, and the CIA, but I can't discuss it on the phone, Wes. Besides Hoover has declared Oswald the lone killer, so the case is closed."

"So you're going to sit on what you know?"

"Are you crazy? The CIA has been working with Giancana, Roselli, Yaras, Ruby, Trafficante, Marcello, Frank Fiorini, and the Cuban exiles. Ruby and Fiorini are running guns and drugs between Miami and Dallas. Trafficante is running drugs and whores from France and he has hit men who hit the hit men. You bet your ass I'm sitting on it."

"Is Fiorini the guy who used to run things in Cuba and then worked for Castro?"

"Yeah. Fiorini is a former crooked cop from Philadelphia. He worked for Giancana in Cuba. He bailed out of Cuba in fifty-nine to save his ass. He's been working for the CIA running guns and drugs all over hell."

"Remember when I told you and Roemer in 1960 about Roselli working with the CIA and some Cuban exiles? Roemer laughed at me. He didn't believe me when I said the CIA was in bed with the Outfit and that they wanted to whack Castro."

"Roemer doesn't believe anything he doesn't hear over a bug. Roselli is another bad-ass. Johnny was Sam's hit man before going to Hollywood and taking over the movie industry. He was in Dallas for the hit but our evidence is like a London fog on a bad day. Hell, the newspapers know more about what's going on down here in Miami than we do. We're still playing catch up just like we did in Chicago in 1959 when we had to read the papers to find out who was in the Mob. Your Cuban friend probably knows more about what is happening with the CIA and the Mob than the FBI does."

CHAPTER 26
Call to Ralph Hill

J. Edgar Hoover had denied that organized crime existed until November 14, 1957, when a New York State trooper discovered that a large group of gangsters held a meeting in Apalachin, New York. The FBI likened the Apalachin discovery to America's discovery by Christopher Columbus in 1492. Hoover's FBI had been investigating the Mafia for only five years by the time Kennedy was assassinated. It is no great mystery that the FBI knew so little about the mob.

Soon after becoming Attorney General Bobby Kennedy visited the New York City FBI Office to observe the FBI in action. He asked Assistant Director in Charge, John F. Malone, whom we called "Cement Head," for the latest information on organized crime.

Malone responded, "I don't know the latest. I haven't read today's paper yet."

I knew that Hill was in a tough spot as the supervisor of organized crime in Miami. He may have received information from some Cuban exiles, but not necessarily so. I asked, "Are you okay?"

"Yes, but this is the big league, Wes. You had better stop talking about Kennedy if you want to keep drinking Cutty. Trafficante has men that could run you off one of those hairpin turns before you could blink."

"Okay! I'll go back to sailing the old clipper ship of 1869."

"You mean you remember the date of that ship?"

"Hey, Ralph, I look at the label every day. Cutty Sark takes its name from the famous clipper, built in Scotland in 1869. It was the fastest sailing vessel of her day."

"Well, I always knew you were a sailor. That's why we asked you and Paula to go out with us on SIX BELLES. Take care Wes. Say hello to Paula."

"Will do. Tell Billie I said hello."

Ralph Hill had just confirmed my worst nightmare. Ralph was a happy, go-lucky agent when we went out drinking in Chicago. We had gone for a one week fishing trip with our wives in 1955. We were the best of drinking buddies. I trusted Hill and he trusted me. Both of us could have been fired if Hoover found out that I let Ralph use my apartment to "interview" Giancana's girl friends to get information from them. To my knowledge no one on the Top Hood Squad knew that Hill was using my apartment, except maybe Maz Rutland, who had used my apartment occasionally for his own conquests. Maz Rutland was transferred to the Bureau in 1966 where he became a unit supervisor for Chicago's Top Hoodlum Program.

The yacht SIX BELLES, about a forty-five foot sailing vessel, belonged to Ralph's friend. I did not ask Ralph what their relationship had been. One day I was invited out on SIX BELLES, named after the owner's six daughters. The owner had invited Ralph Hill, and two other agents, all of whom worked on Chicago's Top Hoodlum Program. None of the agents knew the first thing about a sailboat. I was surprised to see that all the married agents had girl friends along for the ride. I was divorced and so I brought my sailing friend, Paula, because she was an avid sailor. Other than the skipper, Paula and I were the only ones on board who knew how to sail. Paula and I were becoming serious and I could see that she was not the least bit happy about three married FBI agents going sailing with girl friends. She asked me whether all married agents did this sort of thing. Actually I was a bit surprised myself that the other two agents brought girl friends instead of their wives, but then I did not know them as well as I knew Ralph Hill. The women could have been informants for all I knew. I did not ask.

Ralph was unusually blunt when I talked with him about the Kennedy assassination. Hill's message to keep quiet came through to me loud and clear. I suspected that Ralph knew a lot more than I did about the assassination. He had probably learned volumes as the supervisor of the organized crime squad in Miami. I decided not to be a hero or ever try to become a rich man. From what I knew in 1963 I may have been able to write a best seller, but then I most likely would have been dead before the ink dried on the pages.

As an old timer once told me, "discretion is the better part of valor." The older agent had misquoted William Shakespeare, who had written in *Henry IV, Part 1, V, iv,* that, "The better part of valor is discretion."

After talking with Ralph Hill, I was beside myself with curiosity as to what Ramon knew about Kennedy's assassination. I wondered how long we both would live.

Marshall Rutland was later transferred to FBIHQ where he became the Bureau supervisor of the THP. Rutland was a physical fitness buff when I knew him and he was in splendid physical condition. Maz had also used my apartment on North Lake Shore Drive for several interviews of female informants with mob connections.

Maz Rutland died in 1975 at the age of 46.

Ralph Hill had a heart attack in 1976, but survived until 1985 when he died at the age of 57.

Rutland did not live long enough to retire.

When I received word that Rutland and Hill died at such young ages, I wondered just how long I had to live. I was happy to have made it to retirement when I turned 50 in 1977. I wanted to escape the horror of it all.

CHAPTER 27
A Call to Ramon

I called Ramon's old number. A female answered. When she understood who I was she gave me Ramon's private, unlisted, number. After reaching Ramon, I asked him for a pay phone number where I could call him in about an hour. I had driven to the Jenny Wiley State Park Lodge and called from a secure pay phone.

"Buenos Dias, Ramon. Este es Wes Swearingen."

"Bueno. Como esta?"

"Muy bien, E tu?"

"Miedoso. What happened to you?"

"I was transferred to Kentucky. You were in Miami when I left Chicago."

"Por que?"

"Rutina, I guess. Why are you afraid?"

"Remember what I told you last year, what el jefe said?"

"Si."

"It happened like I said it would, didn't it?"

"You mean the team?"

"Si."

"Like a football team?"

"Close. I heard there were four, maybe five, men on the street, and back up, which I told you about."

"Who were they?"

"I heard it was Indio, Roselli, Yaras, Cain, Hunt, Ruby, and Oswald. Jack Ruby was to let Oswald do his thing, to create a diversion just like we trained for in Florida, then take him for a ride and hit him."

"You mean el tonto?" I didn't know the Spanish word for patsy so I said tonto, which means fool.

"Si."

"Are you sure?"

"Was I sure about the Bay of Pigs?"

"I'm sorry, Ramon. The Bay of Pigs was so crazy I thought you were pulling my leg."

"I didn't pull your leg then and I'm not pulling it now. I can't talk anymore. I've told you who did it. Just keep my name out of it. Don't ever call again. Forget you know me, please. The CIA and the Florida guys plan to kill any witness who might open his trap."

"Okay, Ramon. Gracias. Adios."

Ramon clearly was not pleased to get my call. It was probably stupid of me to call him after what Hill had said. However, I felt good that Ramon had trusted me.

CHAPTER 28
A Call to Mike Simon

Mike Simon and I had run one of Fidel Castro's assassins out of Chicago. It is quite possible the assassin was after Ramon. That was the time I learned the word *pendejo,* which was a new Spanish word to me.

"Mike, this is 'pendejo.' How are you?"

Mike laughed and then replied, "Fine. How are you Joven?" Mike was a few years older than I and so he called me Joven, which in Spanish means young man.

"I called Ramon recently. He told me what happened."

Mike answered, "Ramon called me after you were transferred to Louisville. After Dallas he called and told me the what, when and where, just before it was going down, but the bureau thought it was all bullshit. Roemer laughed his ass off because he never heard about it over Mo."

"Oh, shit. Now what?"

"Forget it Joven. What's done is done."

I tried to respond, "But..." Mike cut me off.

"Forget it Joven! You remember Guy Bannister?"

"Yes, he was SAC in Chicago in 1954."

"Bannister is up to his eyeballs in this."

"You're joking."

"No, I'm not joking. You thought Ramon was joking when he mentioned Guy Bannister. Well, Bannister's buddy,

Jack Martin, told the FBI in New Orleans that Bannister and David Ferrie were involved with the CIA."

"What the hell is wrong with Bannister?"

Mike said, "Martin told the FBI that Ferrie was to fly Oswald and the others out of the country."

"The FBI knew this and still Hoover claimed Oswald to be the lone assassin?"

"The FBI thought Martin was a nut case."

"You mean they didn't even bother to check it out?"

"You aren't getting it, Joven. This is big time. If you keep talking about this you will be a dead man. If we meet up again we may be able to talk, but not now. Just forget it. Forget it. Forget it. How is Paintsville?"

"Paintsville is a dry territory. Need I say more?"

"That's horrible."

"I cover six counties and they are all dry. I have to pick up a case or two of Cutty when I go to Louisville."

"You are in a living Hell."

"You got that right."

Mike said, "Hey, Joven, I have to run. Give me a call after things have blown over."

"Will do, so long. Give my best to the missus. I'll keep you in mind on my trips to Louisville."

"So long, Joven. Good luck. Tell Paula I said hello."

Mike Simon was usually fairly calm, cool, and collected. This time he was definitely disturbed about the assassination. I did not see, or talk to Mike Simon again until 1975, after Mike was transferred to Las Vegas, Nevada, and after I was assigned to Los Angeles, California.

The movie *"BONANNO: A GODFATHER'S STORY,"* which aired on Showtime TV on Sunday, July 25 and Monday, July 26, 1999, revealed that the Mafia was behind the Kennedy assassination. It is understood that *Bonanno: A Godfather's Story* is a movie and movies, even when they are a documentary or a biography, often stray from the facts for entertainment purposes. However, if you are to believe any of Bonanno's story that he was actually a Mafia godfather in New York and that he had some semblance of truth that he honored his Mafia family, then you have to believe that the portrayal of the Mafia's part in the Kennedy assassination is somewhat accurate. It would be incredible to believe that Joseph Bonanno, Sr. would allow the killing of JFK to be blamed on the Mafia if this were not actually true. For Joseph Bonanno, Sr. to blame the Mafia for JFK's assassination does not add that much to his movie. I do believe it is true that he can tell the story in 1999 because all of his friends are dead. One part that he did not include in his movie was the CIA's roll in the assassination of John Kennedy. This may be too dangerous a story even for a powerful Mafia don, at the age of 94, to include in his own biography.

CHAPTER 29
The CIA trained the Cubans to bomb America

In 1962, Ramon named several Cuban exiles that were trained by the CIA in Florida in the use of military grade explosives. These anti-Castro men became members of a terrorist group named Alpha 66. The Cuban exiles were friendly toward the United States because they fled Fidel Castro's Cuba and needed a nice quiet place to live, so they settled in Miami, Florida. After being trained by the CIA these desperate Cubans turned against the United States after President Kennedy failed to support them at the Bay of Pigs invasion and so they became terrorists. They used such names as Alpha 66 and Cuban Power. Ramon said some were in the Bay of Pigs invasion in 1961 and had survived capture, or death, as did Ramon.

The bureau transferred me to Kentucky in December 1962 and I arrived on duty at Louisville in January 1963, and so I did not have much use for the names while assigned to Kentucky. The terrorist bombers in Kentucky were coal miners who were fighting the coal mine operators for better wages, an old American custom.

In 1968, Hoover transferred me to New York City. I was given a choice of criminal squads and so I picked the Stolen Car Squad because car ring cases in Kentucky gave me a real high. Because of my success in investigating railroad bombings and attempted coal mine bombings in Kentucky,

I was soon assigned bombing matters, which the car squad also investigated. Many of the agents on the Car Squad were fresh out of Training School at Quantico. They knew nothing about investigating a terrorist bombing case. I had asked my supervisor to assign all bombing matters to me so that I could get a better picture of who the different terrorist groups were during those anti-America days when icons such as John Lennon were inciting young people to riot in the streets.

The Cuban exiles set off several bombs in New York City, but no positive evidence was recovered by the New York City Police Department Bomb Squad connecting the Cubans directly to the bombings. One day, while reading a memorandum from the Los Angeles FBI Office, I discovered that the bombers of the Air France airlines office had left fingerprints on a "Cuban Power" sticker that had been pasted adjacent to the doors. The fingerprints were recovered by the Los Angeles Police Department (LAPD) who did not know about the CIA trained Cuban exiles or the CIA's plan to terrorize America. I sent an AIRTEL to the Los Angeles office requesting that they obtain the "Cuban Power" sticker from the LAPD and send it to the FBI's Latent Fingerprint Division to be compared with fingerprints on file of about a dozen known Cuban exile terrorists. Two of the terrorists were identified through the latent fingerprints found in Los Angeles. The two men who were identified happened to be two of the men Ramon named in 1962.

Two outstanding FBI agents in Miami interviewed Hector M. Cornillot y Llano Jr., then 30, and Juan Garcia-Cardenas, also then 30. Both Hector and Juan admitted their part in several Los Angeles bombings, which included offices of Shell Oil Co.'s computer operations office, two Mexican tourist offices, the ticket offices of Air France and Japan Air Lines, the British consulate, a Beverly Hills travel agency, and the offices of the Socialist Workers Party and the Young Socialist Alliance.

The Cuban exile terrorists had set bombs at ten different locations in New York City. In all, the terrorists set 72 bombs throughout the United States. The chaos was just what the CIA ordered in an effort to create disorder. With all the controlled terrorist activity going on in the United States, the CIA could control the domestic and political scene in America just as they had done for many years in several foreign countries.

Cornillot told the FBI agents that he and Juan Garcia had been trained by the CIA and that the CIA had given them the explosives. Cornillot admitted to the FBI that he had taken part in the ill-fated Bay of Pigs invasion. Cornillot also admitted being a member of "Los Subversivos," an action group of the militant "Cuban Power" organization. Cornillot and Juan Garcia were arrested in Miami on October 28, 1968. They were later tried in Los Angeles where they were convicted and sent to prison.

I later met one of the agents in New York City when he was assigned to the car squad to which I was assigned. FBI rules prohibit me from mentioning his name, but we worked a few stolen cars together in New York City. I have the highest respect for this agent

Later, I met Matt Perez in Los Angeles who had become my supervisor in 1977, just before I retired. If I had known Matt was going to be my supervisor, I may have not retired when I did. I also have the highest respect for Matt Perez

Matt Perez later sued the FBI for its failed policy toward Hispanic agents and won. Matt was promoted to the position of Deputy Associate Director (DAD) of the FBI. The judge who oversaw the suit said the FBI's personnel policy was bankrupt.

The last I heard from Matt was when he was SAC of the Albuquerque office about 1992, when I lived in Santa Fe, New Mexico.

I have often pondered what the outcome of the Kennedy assassination would have been if agents such as R.C. and Matt Perez had held top level positions in 1962 and 1963. It is quite possible that Kennedy may not have been assassinated if Matt Perez had been in charge of the Training and Inspection Division instead of sycophants such as Mark Felt and James Gale.

CHAPTER 30
Operation Solo

For once the FBI got it right.

Two FBI agents in Chicago, Carl Freyman and Walter Boyle, along with the FBI's most important informant in American history, CG-5824-S*, just may have saved the planet Earth from a nuclear war with the Soviet Union. I can now write about CG-5824-S* because the FBI has made public his identity. In the early 1950s, Freyman developed an informant who was operated for a quarter century. The man was unquestionably the greatest informant in the annals of the FBI. His name was Morris Childs; code number CG-5824-S. The CG stood for Chicago. 5824 was the chronological informant number for Chicago. S stood for security. As the importance of CG-5824-S increased, an asterisk was added to the symbol number.

During the time I wrote investigative reports under the supervision of Carl Freyman, Carl insisted that I quote two or more T symbols when reporting information from Morris Childs on high ranking communist party members such as Claude Lightfoot, former Chairman of the Communist Party of Illinois, and Mollie West, former Secretary of the Communist Party of Illinois. Therefore, if I used different bits of information from Morris Childs four times in a report then I identified Morris in the details of the report as T-1, T-2, T-3, and T-4. As the informant's position in the U.S. Communist Party grew, and his association and influence with the Soviet Union increased, Carl Freyman insisted that an asterisk be added to the symbol to further hide the identity from agents in other field offices. An asterisk indicated to all FBI agents that the source was a wire tap or a bug and could not testify in a court of law. Morris Childs eventually became known as CG-5824-S*. If Morris could be identified by the date of the information, when there were only two people in a meeting, then only the month and year were used as the date of receipt of the information. As an in-joke, we agents in Chicago referred to Morris Childs as "24 s-h-h." Outsiders and those at FBI headquarters referred to Morris Childs as 58.

Morris Childs was born in Kiev on June 10, 1902. His name then was Moishe Chilovsky. He came to the United States in 1911 and settled in Chicago with his parents. Morris formally joined the United Communist Party of America at the age of seventeen and fell under the influence of communism and was considered a charter member. Morris strongly supported Joseph Stalin and the Soviets trusted him completely.

The FBI had an interview program which was simple enough. Interview every communist in the Chicago area and someone may talk.

Freyman attempted to enlist in the military during World War II but was turned down because he wore glasses. Carl joined the FBI to serve his country and serve his country he did. Carl made his own niche in the FBI and by the early 1950s he was considered the FBI's authority on communism. He could discuss dialectical materialism with the best of the communists. Freyman talked at length with Morris Childs until Freyman convinced Morris to work for the FBI. It was the greatest coup d'état the FBI had ever made, because Morris was trusted totally and completely by the Soviet Union. After

Freyman developed Morris Childs as an informant, Morris traveled to the Soviet Union annually, starting in 1958, and carried huge sums of money back to the United States for the communist party. As the Soviet Union trusted Morris more and more, the sums of money grew to more than a million dollars in U.S. currency per trip.

CHAPTER 31
Walter Boyle

In sharp contrast to Carl Freyman and his nonmilitary service were Walter Boyle and his outstanding military record during the Korean War. Walt Boyle had been transferred to Chicago under a cloud. Walt had been busted from the position of a Bureau supervisor at headquarters in Washington, D.C. down to a brick agent for his kindness to a married female clerk. The clerk was fired for having sex with a non-FBI married man. Had this clerk been a White Anglo-Saxon male agent she would have, at most, been transferred, but not fired. A Bureau supervisor with a pea-size brain had decided the female clerk, whom he described as a whore, had to go. Walt, a religious married man with children, disagreed with his supervisor. Walt invited the female clerk to his home to have dinner with him and his wife on the Friday that the female clerk was fired, in an effort to sooth her disastrous situation. Walt wanted to show the woman that not every Bureau supervisor was a horse's ass.

Walt was called on the carpet the following Monday by his supervisor and soon thereafter Walt was transferred to Chicago. Other agents in Chicago shunned Walt like a rotten apple, but I invited him out to lunch the day we met. I took Walt to the Men's Grill in the Carson, Pirie, Scott Department Store, located at 1 South State Street, where they served a complete salad bar on Fridays with vegetables, dressings, cheeses, and meats. We were both in our early thirties and so we did not worry about returning to the buffet for a third time.

I liked Walt instantly as he related his story. Walt said, "I was reprimanded like a five-year-old kid. That meat-headed supervisor wagged his finger in my face so many times that I lost my cool."

"What happened?"

Walt said, "I told that bastard, 'You shake your god-damned finger at me one more time and I'll break it off in your ass.' "

I laughed so hard that I almost choked. I said, "That sounds like my confrontation with Joe Culkin over my refusing to investigate people who read library books on communism. I told Culkin to go shove it. I clicked my heels, gave him a Heil Hitler salute, and walked out of his office."

"You're as bad as I am, Wes," replied Walt

"I can't stand that little twerp, Culkin."

Walt asked, "What kind of work do you do?"

"I was on the bag job squad for about five years. I must have been involved in close to 500 bag jobs starting in 1952, many of them with Joe Culkin. Now he's my supervisor and I work Cuban counterintelligence. I've been working Cuban matters since 1957, ever since Fidel Castro came down out of Oriente Province and took over Cuba. What are you doing?"

"Well, I'm lucky, I guess. None of the supervisors wanted me for mouthing off at the Bureau."

"I heard why you were transferred. Congratulations for being nice to the woman who was fired"

"Thank you," replied Walt. "Carl Freyman looked at my military record and figured I deserved another chance."

"I did bag jobs on CP headquarters with Carl Freyman."

Walt looked too young for WW II so I asked, "Were you in the Korean war?"

"Yes. I was a Second Lieutenant attached to a Marine Corps battalion. I was decorated for bravery several times."

"If you don't mind my asking, what did you do?"

"It was crazy, Wes. Once I was in a single-engine plane when the pilot got shot. I didn't know how to fly but I landed the plane without crashing."

"Wow! I'll bet that made you pucker?"

"I got a Bronze Star on the battlefield. Major General Pollack of the 1st Marine Division said I was some kind of hero."

"Was it for landing the plane?" I asked.

"No. I was a forward observer on an outpost about a mile forward of the Main Line of Resistance when the enemy launched a heavy attack. For about a day and a half I was subjected to intense enemy artillery and mortar fire but refused to leave. I called up friendly artillery fire on those North Koreans and we killed about 400 gooks."

I replied, "No wonder Freyman wanted you on his squad. Many of the top Bureau officials are draft dodgers from WW II." Although Walt and Carl had different backgrounds, they had one thing in common. They did not trust the helium-headed supervisors at the Bureau to oversee the case of CG-5824-S*. Many of the Bureau supervisors were promoted because the agents in charge of the various field offices did not want them working in their divisions. A few good guys like Walt slip through the crack now and then and are promoted.

Walt finished his salad and then said, "Freyman said something about handling 5824."

I said, "That is one hell of an honor, Walt. 5824 is Carl's pet baby. He guards Morris with his life."

Walt continued, "Carl said that Jack, 24's brother, is an informant in New York."

"Yes. Jack's symbol number is NY-4309-S*. For a long time, when I wrote reports on top communist figures in Chicago, I thought NY-4309-S* was a wiretap or an illegal black bag job on the Communist Party headquarters in New York City. This is how tightly the FBI guarded the identities of Morris and Jack Childs. Just about any information of importance concerning the Communist Party in New York City comes from NY-4309-S*. I did bag jobs with Carl on CP headquarters but for a long time Carl would not tell me the identity of NY-4309-S*."

Walt and I finished our lunch and returned to the office. When our paths crossed in the office we often had lunch together, if possible.

After leaving Chicago in 1963, I did not see Walt again until 1969.

CHAPTER 32
Gus Hall, Chairman of the CPUSA

Gus Hall was the Chairman of the Communist Party of the United States (CPUSA). Gus Hall was also an informant for the FBI.

I saw Walter Boyle again in 1969 while I was assigned to New York City. Walt had walked through my squad area of the New York City FBI office. When I saw him, I said, "Walt, have you been assigned to New York?"

He flashed a big smile and said, "No. I'm here to see Gus Hall."

"What?" I exclaimed.

Walt repeated, "I'm here to see Gus Hall."

I shook my head. "I might have guessed it. How about lunch?"

Walt looked at his watch and said, "Sure. I'll be back in about fifteen minutes."

(We did not discuss Gus Hall any further. In 1978, a year after I retired, Charles R. Garry, a San Francisco attorney for many left wing radicals, told me that Mrs. Gus Hall told him that Gus Hall was an informant for the FBI.)

I looked at my watch when Walt returned to my desk. "Damn. When you say fifteen minutes, you mean fifteen minutes." Walt had been on time nearly to the second.

"Got a place in mind? Somewhere close? My schedule is tight."

"There is a good Chinese restaurant one block over on Lexington, a Jewish Deli one block North, or an all American hamburger place one block South."

"I can go for some Chinese."

"Good. It is quiet there and we can talk about old times."

We walked over to the Golden Dragon where several agents used to drink their lunch and wait for their car pool to pick them up about 5:30 p.m. One former Chicago agent I had worked with warmed a stool at the bar for several years. One afternoon he was approached by two FBI agents from the Administrative Division, the equivalent of an Internal Affairs in a police department. The agent excused himself while he went to the men's room. When the two agents heard a gunshot, they ran to the men's room and found Forrest Thompson with a bullet hole in his head.

(I have not searched for a death certificate on my late friend Forrest Thompson with whom I had worked in New York City on the Sam Melville bombing case. His death was a shock to all of us throughout the FBI. May his soul rest in peace.)

The Golden Dragon was an upscale Chinese place with gold decor and gold framed pictures hanging on the walls. It had high-back booths, excellent for privacy and confidential conversations. It was a hang out for KGB agents traveling to New York City.

Walt and I ordered one of the luncheon specials, Chop Suey and Pork Fried Rice, my favorite special.

"How's Carl Freyman these days?" I asked.

"Still smoking that damned pipe and hanging in there."

"I thought that pipe of his would have killed him by now, or cause cancer."

"Wes, Carl is as strong as a bull."

"Yeah and just as bullheaded when it comes to CG-5824."

"It's good the Bureau didn't control Morris. We might have had World War III."

"How so?"

"As you may know, 24, or his brother Jack, went to the Soviet Union every year since 1958 and brought back millions of dollars for the CP."

"I never knew how much he brought back to the States. I had heard that he skimmed about 5 percent. That's about $50,000 for himself."

Walt laughed, "Hey, it went to a good cause. Besides it was only commie money."

"Right. Who cares if we rip off Khrushchev?"

Our lunch arrived and we dove in like two hungry Bolsheviks. I asked Walt, "Did 24 know anything about the CIA and the JFK assassination?" I didn't want Walt to know I had suspected the CIA. The Golden Dragon was not the place to discuss the Kennedy assassination.

"Not really, except that the Soviets were trying to blame the CIA and Castro just to stir up trouble. The CIA doesn't have the slightest idea who 24 is. In fact, the CIA offered a quarter a million dollars to buy into the deal. When we refused, they said, 'Name your price.'" We said, "You don't have that much drug money. That pissed off the CIA."

I asked, thinking surely the CIA at least knew about Morris. "After all these years the CIA couldn't guess 24's identity?"

"The CIA's sources in Russia were idiots."

Still confused I asked, "Didn't they know about 24's trips?"

"The Russians had a code name for 24 and the CIA doesn't even know who 24 is."

I shook my head and said, "Unbelievable. It's scary to hear that the CIA is so inept."

Walt responded sharply, "Wes, inept isn't the word for it. We nuked the Soviet's sources after WW II. The KGB did much the same to the CIA's sources. In 1960 the KGB thought the CIA believed that the Pentagon needed another war with the Soviet Union as soon as possible."

Amazed, I asked Walt, "Where did they get that goofy idea?"

"Some KGB nut said the U.S. had the bombers to wipe out the Kremlin."

"Is that why Kennedy stood up to Khrushchev during the 1962 Cuban missile crisis?"

"24 kept us advised of Khrushchev's every thought. 24 knew exactly what Nikita was up to. Khrushchev believed 24 was working only for him, reporting on Kennedy, when all the time 24 was our double agent."

I shook my head, "I always thought Kennedy was playing it a little too tough during the missile crisis."

Walt responded, "Nah! Khrushchev was running a bluff. Remember when he issued a statement that he had rockets that could land on a target 13,000 kilometers away?"

I couldn't remember all the crap Khrushchev spewed forth on TV and so I answered, "Vaguely."

"Khrushchev was jerking Kennedy's chain. 24 told us what Russia had and didn't have, so Kennedy played it like John Wayne. If 24 had been wrong, we would have been in world war three."

I knew that Walt had been walking a tightrope. Trying to change the subject I said, "Have some more rice, Walt."

Walt said, "No thanks. I have to keep my weight desirable."

I laughed and said, "I run a few pounds over, now and then, and when it's time for my physical I go on a diet to lose five pounds. It keeps Hoover happy."

Walt smiled and asked, "What are you working on in New York?"

"I started out with stolen cars and then was given terrorist bombing matters."

Walt responded, "You mean like those CIA trained Cuban bombers?"

"Yes. I helped Los Angeles identify two of the Alpha 66 members through fingerprints. They are in jail now."

"The CIA is a jack-off outfit," said Walt.

"How so?"

"They trade in drugs all over the world thinking they can control the drugs if they are in the know, when all the time BNDD and Customs are running crazy trying to stop drugs from entering the U.S."

(The Drug Enforcement Administration (DEA) was known as the Bureau of Narcotics and Dangerous Drugs, BNDD, from 1968-1973. The DEA is a part of the Department of Justice.)

"Yeah, and we are running around trying to put the CIA trained bombers in jail. The Cuban exiles may have set about ten bombs off right here in New York City in 1968. Every time the bombers return to Miami from a mission they set off a bomb in Miami to let their Alpha 66 friends know they are back in town."

Walt said, "That's what I mean. It's like the CIA is bombing the U.S. to stir up trouble just to keep their jobs."

I asked Walt, "Did you know the CIA trained the Mafia

and the Cuban exiles in Florida to kill Castro? Can you imagine the CIA training the Mafia how to do a hit?"

He replied, "Yes. We heard that after Kennedy was killed."

"Why didn't Hoover come out with the truth about JFK?"

CHAPTER 33
Hoover wanted to be Director for Life

After much studied thought Walt responded, "Because Hoover wanted LBJ to give him a lifetime extension as FBI Director. Hoover and LBJ were good buddies. Hoover knew that the CIA was behind the assassination after confidential sources came forward, but it was then too late to expose what had happened and Hoover would have been embarrassed since he had already proclaimed Oswald the lone assassin. Besides, Hoover could have been hit by the CIA. Hoover has documents in his secret files, which only Helen Gandy (Hoover's lifetime Confidential Secretary) knows about. Hoover keeps the files to blackmail anyone who may try to kick him out of office. Hoover could not admit that the Mafia had killed JFK since he had denied the existence of the Mafia until just five years before JFK was killed. There was no way Hoover would implicate the Cubans and the CIA in JFK's murder."

I said, "I tried to report to the Bureau that a Cuban exile source had warned me of Kennedy's assassination."

Walt exclaimed, "What?"

"S-h-h-h. Not so loud."

Walt whispered, "You knew Kennedy was going to be killed before it happened?"

"Yes. A whole year before it happened. A Cuban exile told me about it. I went to Bill Roemer with the information that the CIA and the Mafia were going to whack Kennedy. Roemer just laughed at me. He told me to get some new sources. And, as a second thought, Roemer said, 'Don't send anything to the Bureau about the Mob hitting Kennedy or we'll all be in shit up to our eyeballs.' "

Walt frowned and said, "It's a good thing you didn't talk to any one other than Roemer. If you had sent that to the Bureau and the CIA heard about it, you and your Cuban friend would be pushing up daises."

"Thanks a lot, Walt."

"I'm serious, Wes. Those CIA bastards are ruthless when it comes to defending their turf."

I asked Walt, "Do you know how many witnesses have been put on a slab since November 22, 1963?"

"Not really." He replied.

"About fifty." I answered. "I heard about the more important ones from newspaper and TV reports. I haven't kept close track. I was in Eastern Kentucky away from the horror of it all."

"A lot of them were Mafia types and CIA operatives."

"It always kind of bothered me that I didn't send something to the Bureau."

"It's a good thing you didn't."

"I was leery to say anything because I once gave information to the CIA about Soviet ships in Havana Harbor. A Cuban exile had photographed Russian ships and gave me the photos. I turned them over to the CIA after obtaining Hoover's permission to do so. The next thing I knew my source was caught and murdered."

"You have to be careful when dealing with those CIA guys. They are dangerous. They don't think twice about assassinating someone. They do it all over the world and think it's fun. They probably thought Kennedy deserved killing because he worked out a deal with Khrushchev that shut down the CIA's Operation Mongoose."

(The CIA had undertaken a massive program to overthrow Fidel Castro. The program was called Operation Mongoose, after the ferret-like animal that kills cobras and other venomous snakes. The CIA had designated the Mongoose unit as Task Force W. They were to carry out Kennedy's secret war against Castro. No time, money, effort—or manpower was to be spared. President Kennedy did not consult with the CIA before Kennedy promised Soviet Prime Minister Khrushchev that Operation Mongoose would be halted. That made the CIA mad as hell. It also made the Mafia and the Cuban exiles about as mad as a stirred up batch of Africanized bees.)

I said, "My source said they were mad as hell over that. So were the Cuban exiles and the Mafia."

Walt looked at his watch. "Hey. It's been great. I've got to catch a subway."

"Yeah, I've got to get back to the office. It was good to see you again, Walt. Take care."

CHAPTER 34
Soviet Order of the Red Banner

Oliver "Buck" Revell, a former top FBI official claims in his 1998 book, written with Dwight Williams, that he, (Revell), "directed or participated in virtually every major FBI investigation—including the JFK assassination, from 1964 to 1994." The problem with Revell's statement about JFK is that Kennedy was killed in 1963 and Hoover had declared the case closed long before Revell joined the FBI. Buck states in his book that he did not have to supervise the "Childes" [sic] brothers when he became ASAC of the Chicago FBI office. The problem with that statement is that Jack lived in New York City, so there was no way Buck could supervise Jack.

The FBI was instrumental in causing Geronimo Pratt, an innocent man, to serve twenty-five years in prison. After being released, Pratt sued the FBI and the Los Angeles Police Department and won a $4.5 million dollar settlement in 2000. This must have been a major case for the FBI. Where was Revell during all those years if he "directed or participated in virtually every major FBI investigation?"

The supervisors at Bureau headquarters had decided years ago to let the Chicago and New York agents run with the ball in Operation Solo. There is no way the Bureau would have allowed any ASAC, such as Buck Revell, who was assigned to the criminal division of Chicago, to touch Operation Solo with a ten-foot pole. However, Buck Revell had nothing to supervise in 1975 because Operation Solo had already been revealed to Senator Frank Church. It was no longer a top-secret spy case. Former President Ronald Reagan agreed to honor Morris Childs at the White House when he learned of the spy case. Soon the whole operation was spilled to the public as "Operation Solo."

The Soviet Union awarded Jack Childs the Order of the Red Banner in 1975, which is given only to those who distinguish themselves in battle.

Jack Childs died on August 11, 1980, at the age of seventy-three. The FBI believes that if it had not been for Jack's support and encouragement, Morris would not have been able to carry out Operation Solo.

Jack and Morris Childs had made a total of fifty-seven missions to the Soviet Union on behalf of the FBI. They had transported nearly $30 million in U.S. currency from the Soviet Union to the U.S. in support of the Communist Party of the United States, but communism still collapsed. Walt had met Morris Childs at the airport each time he brought in millions of dollars. Even when 24's plane was late, Walt was there to guide him through U.S. Customs. The FBI had won the war against the Soviet Union.

Morris Childs died in Chicago on June 2, 1991. He was eight days shy of his ninetieth birthday. Although he risked his life, he made out well financially. His annual salary was double that of an FBI agent. The 5 percent that he skimmed from the approximately $30 million he brought from Russia netted him $1.5 million.

Walt Boyle, a dedicated husband, father, U.S. Marine and FBI agent, reportedly died in 1996. May he rest in peace.

The citizens of this country, and of the world, owe their gratitude to Carl Freyman, Walter Boyle, Morris Childs and Jack Childs.

I often wonder what the outcome of the Kennedy assassination would have been if FBI agents such as Carl Freyman and Walter Boyle had been involved in the investigation. What would have happened if Freyman had known in 1962 about the CIA's plan to kill Kennedy? Carl Freyman told Hoover that he, Freyman, must control CG-5824-s* and Hoover listened. Since Freyman was not one of Hoover's fawning bootlicks such as Gale and Felt, and was not afraid to stand up to Hoover, it is quite possible that Freyman could have overruled Hoover's decision to proclaim Lee Harvey Oswald as the lone assassin.

CHAPTER 35
Las Vegas 1975

I went to Las Vegas just before Christmas for a vacation and to visit with my old working partner and drinking buddy, Mike Simon, who had been transferred to Las Vegas, Nevada. Mike reminded me a little of the actor Ernest Borgnine with the broad welcoming smile much like Bill Roemer, only Mike's smile was intentional where as Roemer's smile was more like "What do I do now folks?"

Simon had worked bank robberies in Chicago before being assigned to work Cuban matters. Simon spoke Tex-Mex and so he was perfect for the Cuban assignments. He got along well with Joseph Culkin at first because Mike's older brother, Bill Simon, was a SAC and well liked by Hoover.

The first time I worked with Mike he put me on the spot. We went to a Discount Liquor Store in Chicago's Downtown area known as the Loop and bought a bottle of Cutty Sark Scotch Whisky. Then we went to my North Lake Shore Drive apartment to discuss Cuba and Fidel Castro. Up until then I had been a gin martini drinker, but I was instantly converted to scotch, which did not give me a headache or hangover.

Another time Mike completely fooled me when he invited me to meet his "informant." We checked out of the office and went directly to a quiet lounge on the edge of the Loop near Wabash Avenue. After Mike ordered a Cutty on the rocks I asked, "I thought we were going to see your informant?"

Mike answered, "This is my informant."

From then on Mike Simon and I were the best of partners.

During my visit to Las Vegas, Mike took me to Caesar's Palace where he had some confidential sources and where I met another "informant." After taking a sip of the Cutty Sark on the rocks, I asked Mike, "What kind of work are you doing in Las Vegas?"

"What else? I'm working the mob."

"That beats Cuban matters."

"Sure does. How about you?"

"I'm working the Weatherman Underground Organization. We call it WUO. Bernardine Dohrn is the Chairman and CEO. She is the one who spells America with a K."

"Wasn't she in that townhouse explosion in New York City in 1970?"

"Quite possibly. Kathy Wilkerson and Kathy Boudin were seen running down the street. Boudin was bare-ass naked."

I changed the subject. "Did you hear about Maz Rutland?"

"Sure did. What a shocker. He was only about 45 or 46 and in perfect condition."

"Maz used my apartment in Chicago for some interviews. I wonder whether that or his position at the bureau had anything to do with his death."

Mike replied, "Quite possibly. E. Howard Hunt has been neutralizing a lot of potential witnesses. Maybe Hunt wanted to get to Rutland before Rutland was called to testify?"

"That's scary." I took another long drink of scotch. "A lot of potential witnesses have been murdered, or have died of ACCIDENTAL DEATH."

"About seventy individuals with connections to the JFK assassination have been whacked. Oswald was the first to die." Mike sipped his scotch. "I told you a few years ago that this was something to forget."

"I never thought it would get this bad."

"It will get worse before it gets better. Some of the big shot guys like Giancana and Roselli may be called to testify. I'll bet a long one they are rubbed out before they take the witness stand"

"How is Ralph Hill doing?"

"Ralph is still hanging in there as far as I know."

"Ralph did a lot of interviews in my apartment, including Judy Campbell."

"No shit. I didn't know that."

"I wanted Ralph to keep that quiet. Hoover may have had a fit if he knew Ralph was using my apartment to interview mob girl friends and wives."

"You were skating on pretty thin ice my friend."

"Tell me about it. When Ralph and Maz first asked for my keys I thought they just wanted to hang out, or have a quick fling. I had no idea their penetrating interviews were mob related until after the fact. Then it was too late to stop. I just prayed a lot."

Mike replied, "You're one lucky son-of-a-bitch that it blew over."

I asked, "I wonder what Bill Sullivan will say if he is called to testify, now that Hoover is dead?"

Mike replied, "Bill Sullivan may just spill the whole can of beans."

"Hey, who was that guy from Oklahoma who got bumped off right after Ruby hit Oswald? Ramon never said anything about mob guys in Oklahoma being involved with the CIA."

Mike said, "That was Jack Zangretti. He got popped early. About a month after Oswald."

I asked, "Why"

"Zangretti had a mob-connected gambling outfit near Lake Lugert, Oklahoma, northwest of Dallas. I don't know how he heard about Ruby, but my sources have said that Zangretti told some friends that Jack Ruby was going to pop Oswald."

"You're kidding?"

"Nope! And, sure enough Zangretti was found belly up in Lake Lugert with multiple gunshot wounds, typical gangland style."

CHAPTER 36
Mike on a Roll

Mike was on a roll and so I asked a question that had been on my mind. "What did you hear about Irv Kupcinet's daughter?"

Mike said, "I met Kup once in Chicago. Nice guy. His daughter Karyn supposedly said something before November 22 about Kennedy being killed. She was found in her apartment murdered. I never heard exactly what happened."

"Wow!"

Mike asked, "Did you hear about the news reporter?"

"No."

"Yeah, Bill Hunter, a reporter, supposedly met with Jack Ruby's attorney and some other guys in Ruby's apartment right after Ruby shot Oswald. Hunter was accidentally shot dead in the press room of the Long Beach Police Department about five months later. I built the gun vault in Chicago where all of the rifles, shotguns, and Thompson Sub-machine guns, etc. were stored. Of all the weapons I've handled I never heard of anyone accidentally being shot in the heart from a weapon falling on the floor. If the weapon was a Colt or a Smith and Wesson there is no way it could have been an accident."

"Man, I don't think I want to hear anymore."

"Did you hear about Underhill?"

"Who is he?"

"Not is, was. John Underhill was a CIA agent. He reportedly claimed the CIA was behind the Kennedy assassination. He was found dead in May 1964, shot to death. It was ruled a suicide."

I said sarcastically, "Yeah, sure."

Mike said, "Another reporter, Jim Koethe, who met with Ruby's attorney and Bill Hunter, died in September, 1964, from a chop to the neck."

"Jesus, Mike. Why doesn't the FBI do something?"

"The top brass doesn't want to do anything. There are too many informants involved with JFK. Your informant Ramon for one. You know that for a fact. Then we have Bill Roemer's informant, Richard Cain, who worked with the Cubans and the CIA. Guy Bannister was informing on Oswald when I worked the Fair Play for Cuba Committee. Carlos Marcello was cooperative. There was no way Hoover would admit he had guilty knowledge of a conspiracy, or that he was forewarned that Kennedy was going to be whacked. Hoover has spoken and that is that. Besides, the murder of a President is not a federal violation."

"Are we going to let rogue agents in the CIA get away with killing President Kennedy? That's treason."

"You know the bureau will go to any length to protect an informant, even if it means putting innocent men in jail. Look what they did in Boston."

"Tell me about it. Los Angeles put an innocent Black Panther in jail for life just to protect Julius Butler who lied through his teeth under oath, and the bureau knew about it. In fact my supervisor at the time bragged about closing the informant file so that Butler could honestly say he was not an informant for the FBI. Butler's informant file was re-opened after Pratt was convicted. So now we have the CIA trying to get away with killing Kennedy?"

"They already have. Relax, keep your mouth shut and enjoy your Cutty. You're coming up for retirement."

"Yeah, 1977."

Mike changed the subject completely to Las Vegas and the shows in town. Mike set me up with dinner and a show, which was all on the cuff. I never talked to Mike Simon again because he died in 1994 supposedly of natural causes.

CHAPTER 37
Dallas Oilmen and the JFK Assassination

Not long after the FBI raided my boat on December 14, 1978, in Marina Del Rey, California, which made me known world-wide, I received a letter from a Texas man who said he knew who had killed President Kennedy. After talking with him by telephone I decided to talk with him in person and so I flew to Dallas, Texas.

It was a sunny day in Dallas and much like the weather in Los Angeles. Rain the day before had settled the Texas dust. I scanned the state map provided by the California Automobile Association. My trip to the back country reminded me of the days in Eastern Kentucky when I maneuvered unfamiliar roads with county maps, which actually displayed buildings such as schools, post offices, libraries and other government buildings.

The gentleman I had sought to interview lived among the tumbleweeds and cactus about an hour's drive South of Dallas. The state map was of great help until I turned off the state-maintained road. As I hit the dusty, washboard, dirt road, I was happy that I had rented a car at the airport and was not driving my personal car. The washboard roads again reminded me of the back roads of Kentucky. The best way to locate someone in a rural area is to ask the Postmaster, who usually operates the post office from inside a small general store. The stores in these areas are easy to spot because they fly an American flag on the building. It was always good to see the American flag flapping in the wind atop a rural building.

I stopped and spoke with one Postmaster who gave me directions down the dirt road, turning left here and right there. I had been told to look for a big house surrounded by trees, just beyond the "big tree" next to the road. By the time I arrived at the house I began to think I had made a mistake in coming all the way from Los Angeles just to talk to this fellow who said he knew who had killed Kennedy. It was a relief to hear that he did not think Oswald killed JFK, but that Oswald was just a patsy set up by the CIA and the Mafia.

I pulled up to the house, which had no driveway. The road, the yard, and the driveway were all in one. All dirt. I parked in what looked like the yard and waited a moment for the dust to clear before opening the car door. The house was a two-story, old Victorian style structure. It was probably beautiful in its day, but it now needed some TLC and a good paint job.

A tall, scruffy man, who appeared to be in his seventies, wearing knee-high leather boots, a tailored tan shirt and bush trousers tucked into his boots, greeted me on the porch. I introduced myself and we shook hands. The lanky old man had a grip like the jaws of a tiger. He carried himself as though he could wrestle a steer to the ground in record time. He invited me inside and offered me a seat in a sturdy ranch style wood chair. The living room resembled a disheveled office. The entire first floor looked like a major newspaper room that had just suffered an earthquake of 7.5 on the Richter scale. Newspaper clippings and books were everywhere. The gentleman, whom I'll call Jake Lode, to protect his family's privacy, looked as though he had spent his life working outdoors. His skin was like alligator hide.

Jake said, "Let's go in the dining room. Would you like a sandwich?"

"Thank you, no. I had lunch in Dallas."

"How about some coffee?"

"Yes, please. No cream, no sugar." I had learned, when working in the hot climate of Mississippi as a new FBI agent, that coffee in strange places was safer without cream or sugar.

"Did you have any trouble finding my place?"

"Not really. I'm used to driving strange roads with maps and the help of the local postmaster."

Jake pointed to another room where a young man in his twenties was typing away on an electric typewriter. Jake said, "He's typing a manuscript."

"Are you writing a novel?"

"No. I'm researching the Kennedy assassination."

I said, "It looks as though you have done a lot of work," as I glanced around the room. "You wrote in your letter that you knew who killed Kennedy. Do you know who helped Oswald kill President Kennedy?"

"Texas oilmen. They financed the CIA, the Cubans, and the Mafia."

I didn't have any appointments for the rest of the day so I decided to pacify Jake. "What makes you think that Texas oil was behind the assassination?" This was a new twist that I had not heard.

"I was an oil engineer all my life. I have a degree in geology. I worked on drilling rigs all over the world. I know these Texas oil folks like the back of my hand. They're as crooked as a dog's hind leg."

"If they wanted Kennedy out of the way aren't you afraid they might go after you if you publicly accuse them?"

"I'm too old to care what they do to me. Besides, I'm still good with a gun and I've got several stashed here and there. I want the folks to know how dirty Texas oil really is. They control the whole state from the governor on down. They control how people vote. And, if they can't control the votes, they put a head tax on the voters they don't want counted. They control parts of Washington, the way they controlled Texas when Lyndon Johnson was senator."

Jake's eyes burned right through me. I'd hate to have him mad at me. I asked, "Did you ever file a complaint with the Board of Elections?"

Jake laughed and said, "No use. Big oil controls the election board, too."

"Who is big oil?"

"The biggest guy is the one with the Midas touch, Clinton Murchison, Sr. He was connected with Lady Bird and Lyndon Johnson, Billy Sol Estes, Governor John Connally, Bobby Baker, and the Hunts. He's even in with hoods like Joe Civello and Sam Giancana. These folks were all behind Kennedy's assassination, even the FBI."

I replied, "That's...ah...sounds wild. Is Civello the guy who was at Apalachin in 1957?"

"Yes. Civello was the Dallas Mafia boss then. He was thick with Trafficante and Marcello in Miami."

After looking at the man's house, seeing his papers scattered all over the place and hearing that Lady Bird Johnson and LBJ, and Governor Connally, and the FBI were behind Kennedy's murder, I decided my trip to Dallas was a complete waste of time and money.

I knew the FBI was not in on the killing of Kennedy, but I did not know about the other folks. However, I wanted to learn more about Texas big oil business so I lead Jake along. "Who else is big in Texas oil?"

"You've heard of the Hunts?"

"Yes. Tell me about them." Jake went into his oil field background and his engineering experiences. There were times when I struggled to stay awake. I tightened my leg and butt muscles in a fashion proposed by the late body builder Charles Atlas, who had developed an exercise program called Dynamic Tension. It consists of working one muscle against another, without using weights. It is a great way to fight fatigue, especially when driving a car. I yawned as Jake finally got around to the Hunts.

"The Hunts are right up there on the top of the list with Texas oilmen who wanted Kennedy dead."

Jake's statement brought me to attention. I asked, "May I have more coffee?"

He replied, "Certainly." Then he called to a middle-age Hispanic woman in the kitchen, who had poured the first cup of coffee. "Rosa! More coffee, please."

The woman smiled as she poured my coffee. I said, "Thank you." Rosa then disappeared into the kitchen and closed the door behind her.

"The Hunts are major hitters in Texas oil. Now, there is a whole family who hated Kennedy. The reason I said the FBI is also in on the murder is because a former FBI agent by the name of Paul Rothermal, was chief of security for Hunt Oil in Dallas."

CHAPTER 38
Murchison and Hoover

Jake had now grabbed my attention. This was a new twist. "Go on."

"Nelson Hunt and others put a black-bordered ad in the *DALLAS MORNING NEWS* on November 22, 1963, which was unduly critical of the Kennedy administration."

"That's odd. An ad with a black border in the paper the day Kennedy is killed? Sounds like a funeral espy."

"Not surprising. H.L. Hunt, Nelson's father, said just before Kennedy's visit to Dallas that, "there was no way left to get these traitors out of our government except by shooting them out."

"Whoa! Aside from Rothermal being a former FBI agent, what other ties did the FBI have to big oil?"

"The FBI's two top dogs."

"Top dogs?"

"Murchison was an old pal of J. Edgar Hoover and Clyde Tolson, the two homosexuals."

Jake's story was now becoming a little wild and possibly hateful. I had heard about Murchison. Stories about Hoover and Tolson being gay were not new. I asked, "How so?"

"You have heard about Hoover's trips to Del Mar in California?"

"Every FBI agent knew about the Del Mar parties. Where does Murchison come in?" It was rumored within the FBI that

Hoover and Tolson took vacations at Murchison's place in Del Mar, which were all on the cuff.

"Did you know Murchison owned the Del Charro Motel in Del Mar where Edgar and Clyde stayed?"

I hesitated, "Yes, I heard rumors that Hoover and Tolson had vacationed there every year." I had heard rumors inside the FBI about Hoover and Tolson taking trips to a place in California owned by someone named Murchison, but it didn't really mean much at this point in time. Hoover and Tolson were dead and buried.

"Hoover and his lover, Clyde Tolson, used to go to Del Charro and Murchison picked up the tab. Murchison was connected with Jimmy Hoffa, the Teamsters, and Bobby Baker. Hoover accepted favors from Murchison even though the Senate and the FBI were investigating Murchison's dealings with Baker."

"Can you document this?" I was curious as to how Jake knew so much about Hoover.

"It's right here in the Senate Hearings, newspaper clippings, and William Turner's book *HOOVER'S FBI.*"

Jake showed me one source after the other. I remembered reading Turner's book. Jake handed me *HOOVER'S FBI.* Then it hit me. I remembered Turner writing about Murchison. I hadn't connected the name Clint Murchison when Jake first mentioned his name. "Now I remember. That lying bastard. All those years that Hoover denied there was organized crime and he was taking vacations in Del Mar that were paid for by Mafia connections. What a hypocrite. No wonder Hoover covered up the Kennedy assassination. He's as crooked as a rattle snake." I began to get the picture. There had been rumors inside the FBI about the parties at Murchison's mansion with Hoover, Tolson, LBJ, Bobby Baker, Billy Sol Estes, and other slime balls. Hoover was as dirty as a wildcat rigger.

Jake flashed a huge smile. "Now, do you believe me?"

"Absolutely. But how do you prove it without getting yourself killed? A dozen witnesses were killed just last year."

"Many of the players are dead such as Murchison, who died in 1969. Then there is Hoover who died in 1972. Of course David Ferrie, a CIA operative who was supposed to whisk Oswald out of the state after Kennedy was killed. Jim Garrison, the New Orleans prosecutor, investigated Ferrie and as soon as Ferrie told Garrison that he was involved in Kennedy's assassination Ferrie said, 'I'm a dead man.' Ferrie died in 1967 soon after Garrison made public Ferrie's name."

"I wonder how Garrison felt."

"Probably not too good. Garrison thought Ferrie had been poisoned, but he couldn't prove it because the coroner didn't take any blood samples."

"Who else was involved?"

"Jack Ruby, of course. Guy Bannister, a retired FBI agent who worked with David Ferrie. Jimmy Hoffa, who wanted Kennedy dead. Dorothy Hunt, wife of the CIA guy and Watergate burglar, E. Howard Hunt, was killed in a plane crash in December 1972. She was supposedly going to blow the whistle on her husband. Chicago mob boss Sam Giancana was shot to death in 1975. Sam's trigger man Johnny Roselli was butchered in Florida in August 1976. Then we have mob hit man Charles Niccoletti who had ties with Giancana and Roselli. The press reported that Niccoletti had approval from the CIA to smuggle prostitutes from Marseilles, France, into the U.S. to staff Mafia bordellos in Las Vegas and other mob owned cities. Here is a clipping."

I said, "Guy Bannister was SAC of Chicago in 1954 while I was there. How did you get so many clippings?"

Jake replied, "I started as a kid traveling around drilling for oil. I was impressed with big money. It was a hobby. After I got to know these people I continued to follow their lives through news stories. This place is a mess because I'm trying to make a file on everyone."

"It sounds like you have a Who's Who in the mortuary."

"I haven't told you about my friend George S. de Mohrenschildt, who died in March 1977, with a gunshot to the head."

"Who was George de Mohrenschildt?" I asked, hoping to hear what Jake knew from his life in the oil business.

"He's another big oil man. Or was. I used to work for him. I worked for all of these oil men at one time or another. They said de Mohrenschildt committed suicide. I knew George like a brother. That is like saying Kennedy shot himself at Dealey Plaza."

"I think I remember hearing about him. Tell me more."

"De Mohrenschildt was CIA at one time. George came from Russia. He had connections at the top. He was a geologist, like me, and he hit it big. In 1945 he became owner of the Cuban-Venezuelan Oil Trust Company. He rose to the circle of friends like the Hunts, Murchison, and others. In 1962 he opened an office in Dallas and became a member of the Dallas Petroleum Club. George somehow got to know Oswald. He later introduced Oswald to another CIA type named Ruth Paine. I think George may have been working on Oswald as a patsy for the CIA and the Mob."

CHAPTER 39
Oswald and George de Mohrenschildt

The more Jake talked the stranger his story became. I had a philosophy when in the FBI and working complaint duty. That is the office duty of listening to calls on the telephone and people who walk into the office with some very weird stories. I could usually tell after about five or ten minutes when a person was crazy. Some times the smoother ones took longer to snag.

I had been listening to Jake for two hours and he hadn't cracked once. He was on the edge a few times but never over the hill. I knew that the CIA was working with the Mafia and the Cuban exiles, but I had not heard about the CIA working with Oswald. There had been disinformation stories circulated by the KGB that Oswald was working with the CIA. Jake's story about George de Mohrenschildt did not sound like a disinformation fable from the KGB. Jake knew George and should have had inside information.

I asked Jake, "Do you think Oswald was trying to tell George something?

"How do you mean?"

"Psychiatrists say that people often seek help, unconsciously, when they have an urge to do something bad, like suicide. They give signals that often are not perceived."

Jake replied, "Could be. I thought George was trying to help a mixed up kid."

I said, "Did you know that Oswald had warned the FBI about Kennedy's assassination?"

"The FBI denied that," replied Jake.

"Did you know that James Hosty was trying to develop Oswald as an informant?"

Jake said, "I have it right here where Hoover denied Oswald was ever an FBI informant."

I laughed and said, "I know that's what Hoover told the Warren Commission. Hoover lied through his teeth."

"Did Hoover lie?"

"Lie? That son of a bitch lied ever since he took over as director of the FBI."

"Why would he lie about Oswald?"

"He had to cover himself. Secret Service should have been alerted to Oswald. It was largely the FBI's fault that Kennedy was killed. I'm not saying the FBI did it, I'm saying they did nothing to prevent it."

"Does the FBI always lie about informants?"

I explained, "Yes, except when they are called to testify in court. Otherwise the FBI will deny that anyone is an informant for fear that other informants will become scared that their identity will be revealed and stop giving information to the FBI. The FBI will lie to protect an informant even if it means innocent men will go to jail."

"Your idea that Oswald may have been reaching out for help is interesting."

"I'm not trying to defend Oswald, but Oswald is not the first FBI informant to shoot at a president."

"Can you tell me of another case?"

"Sure. Do you remember Sara Jane Moore who took a shot at Gerald Ford in September 1975 in San Francisco?"

"Yes. I remember that case. I have the news clipping here somewhere."

I answered, "Don't bother." Jake had already given me a handful of news clippings.

"It's here if you need to look at it."

"Moore was not what the FBI called an informant, but the FBI did have a file on her and she was under development. I think she was reaching out for help and the FBI agent who talked to her did not take up on her cry for help. You notice she did not kill Ford; she just shot in his direction. As I recall, I'm not sure she even hit him. Ford probably did more damage to his body when he banged his head walking in and out of helicopters and airplanes."

Jake said, "I think a former Marine hit her gun just as she aimed at Ford, which deflected the shot."

"I had forgotten that." Jake not only had a vice grip but he had a memory like a bear trap.

"If Oswald did tell Hosty that Kennedy was going to be assassinated, why didn't Hosty do something?"

I wanted to explain. I said, "Well, maybe he didn't believe Oswald. After all, he has been characterized as mixed up and a little crazy. Crazy people say crazy things. You would be surprised at the number of nutty complaints the FBI gets every day from all over the country. If the FBI followed up on all nutty complaints it would not get anything else done. When I worked bombing cases in New York City from 1968 to 1970, the NYPD occasionally had days when they received five hundred bombing complaints."

Jake asked, "Shouldn't the FBI have passed Oswald's info to Secret Service so they could worry about it?"

"Yes. Actually, the FBI should have put Oswald on the

Security Index and alerted Secret Service the year before when he was active in the Fair Play for Cuba Committee."

"If Secret Service had been advised of a possible attempt on Kennedy's life in Dallas they could have just put on the glass bubble top and Kennedy would be alive today."

"Maybe, maybe not. In 1954, the FBI was alerted to plans of the Nationalist Party of Puerto Rico (NPPR) to shoot up the U.S. Congress. On March 1, 1954, even with the FBI's massive surveillance of the NPPR, the Puerto Rican nationalists shot and wounded U.S. Congressmen on the floor of the U.S. House of Representatives."

Jake asked, "Were you on surveillance?"

"Yes. They had twenty-four hour surveillance in Chicago. So if the CIA and some Texas oilmen were bent on killing Kennedy, as you claim, it may have been just a matter of time until JFK was whacked—-Mafia style. Maybe Hosty told Hoover and Hoover demanded corroboration. Maybe Hosty couldn't verify Oswald's information in time to prevent the assassination. It would have been difficult for Hosty to corroborate the information. Remember, you said this was a CIA covert operation which the FBI knew nothing about."

"Hoover testified before the Warren Commission that Oswald was not an informant, but that is not what Waggoner Carr, who was the Texas attorney general, told the Warren Commission in January 1964."

"I heard that Carr had a good reputation."

Jake said, "I'd believe Carr before I'd believe Hoover. The fact that Oswald was an FBI informer was leaked to the press. The *Houston Post* ran an article by Lonnie Hudkins on January 1, 1964. I have the article right here."

"What did Carr say?"

"Carr had talked with Allan Sweatt, the chief of the criminal division of the Dallas Sheriff's office. Carr claims the FBI had given Oswald informant symbol number 179."

"There is something wrong with that number. I'm not questioning Carr's integrity, just the information. If Oswald had an informant symbol it would be something like DA-179-S."

"Carr claims Oswald was being paid $200.00 a month."

I explained the FBI's informant program. "Well, if it ever reached a total of more than $400, then Dallas would have been compelled to notify the Bureau of Oswald's informant status. If Oswald had actually been given the symbol number of 179 then the Bureau would have been advised of the number. The rules and regulations are very strict regarding informants."

Jake asked, "Do you believe Oswald was a paid informant?"

"That's possible, but Oswald's information had to be good for him to get $200 a month. SAC Gordon Shanklin could have authorized up to $400, but any amount over $400 would have to have been authorized by Bill Sullivan, assistant director in charge of the Domestic Intelligence Division."

Jake said, "I don't know that Carr ever stated a total of how much Oswald was paid."

"There was something behind Hoover telling Shanklin and Shanklin telling Hosty to destroy FBI documents. We will never know the truth because Hoover, Shanklin, and Hosty all lied about Oswald, under oath."

"It was Hoover's idea to destroy the file, according to Bill Sullivan, but we will never know because Sullivan was shot to death just days before he was scheduled to testify before the House Select Committee on Assassinations in 1977."

I said, "These were not the only documents destroyed soon after Kennedy was killed. I have heard estimates ranging from a few dozen to over a hundred. It isn't the first time the FBI destroyed documents in the face of adversity."

"You mean the FBI has destroyed important documents before?"

I said, "It was rumored within the FBI, after James Hosty was given a disciplinary transfer to Kansas City, which was the FBI's equivalent of Siberia, that Hosty confided in a co-worker that he had developed Oswald as an informant and that he had paid Oswald for information."

Jake said, "Wow! I didn't know that."

"I do not know that the FBI destroyed any files before 1963, but I do know that files were destroyed when the Department of Justice was investigating the illegal Weathermen break-ins in 1977. Thousands of documents at the Bureau were destroyed by the then Weatherman Supervisor and former head of the FBI internal security section, Bob Shackelford, at the direction of Edward S. Miller, who was then assistant director of the Domestic Intelligence Division. The FBI not only destroyed government documents, but I have personal knowledge that two top officials obstructed justice, Elmer Linberg, SAC in Los Angeles, and Andy Decker, ADIC of the Computer Systems Division."

(It is noted that Edward Miller and Mark Felt were later prosecuted for their part in authorizing illegal break-ins against the Weatherman Underground Organization.)

Jake replied, "I guess the FBI is loaded with corruption?"

"You got that right. Not to change the subject, but can you tell me more about corrupt oilmen in Texas?"

CHAPTER 40
George Bush Senior

Absolutely. Have you heard of George Bush?"

I laughed, "You mean the Navy pilot who was shot down during WW II, went to Yale, and later became a Texas congressman?"

Jake replied, "That's the one. He is a transplant from Connecticut. He came down here and started the Zapata Offshore Petroleum Corporation with borrowed money in 1953."

"Smart dude."

"Yeah. He knew nothing about the oil business. Zapata Offshore Company was developed as a subsidiary of Zapata Petroleum Company and it manufactured offshore drilling equipment. George was ZOC's president from 1956 to 1964. In 1966 he became the first Republican to represent Houston in Congress."

"Sounds like he had good connections?"

Jake said, in a slow drawl, "Yep. In 1970, Bush ran for the Senate at the suggestion of Richard Nixon, but Bush lost. As a reward for running, Nixon appointed Bush as the top United States delegate to the UN."

"It helps to have friends in high places."

Jake said, "While Bush was defending the official United States policy of support for both the People's Republic of China and the Nationalist government of Taiwan, the US government was establishing closer ties with Communist China."

"What a hypocrite."

Jake continued, "In 1973, Nixon named George Bush as chairman of the Republican National Committee. Bush was strongly supportive of Nixon during the Watergate scandal."

"It sounds like a good-old-boys club."

"After Nixon resigned and Gerald Ford became president, Ford gave Bush his pick of assignments. Bush chose to be the liaison officer with the People's Republic of China."

"Wasn't that a first?"

Jake replied, "Yes. Then in January 1976 Bush became director of the CIA. He resigned last year to consider entering the 1980 presidential campaign." (It is that Ronald Reagan won the election in 1980 and George Bush became his vice-president in 1981. In 1989, George Bush became President. For the first time in 60 years an outgoing President was succeeded by a member of his own party through an election. At a cost of $30 million dollars, Bush's inauguration was the most expensive in the nation's history. Bush's choice for secretary of defense, John G. Tower, an old Texas crony, was discredited for improper behavior in both professional and private affairs.)

I asked, "Do you think the Texas oilmen were behind Bush?"

"Does a bear shit in the woods?"

"Do you have anything else on the oilmen?"

Jake said, "I heard a rumor that Hoover met with LBJ, Nixon, Sam Giancana and E. Howard Hunt at Clint Murchison's Mansion on the evening of November 21, 1963, to finalize the decision to proceed with the assassination."

I responded, "That rumor is nonsense. I was at Quantico for two weeks of In-service training and on the last day, which was the day Kennedy was shot, I was in Washington. As far as I know Hoover was in D.C. not Dallas the day before."

"Are you sure about that?"

"I'm not positive, but one thing agents always knew about Hoover was his itinerary when he left Washington. Field agents were scared to death of Hoover when he traveled. Just to be on the safe side agents got their hair cut and shoes polished. Some went so far as to go out and buy a new snap brim hat. I remember one time Hoover traveled to Chicago. There were about 275 agents assigned to Chicago at the time, but I was the only agent in the office because I had to dictate an important report. One agent went home and hid under the bed, he was so afraid to meet Hoover."

Jake asked, "Did Hoover go to the Chicago office?"

"Yes. He and Clyde came up to where I was dictating and shook my hand and the hand of my stenographer."

"How was your hair?"

"I had my hair cut the day before Hoover arrived in Chicago. I shined my shoes that morning just to be on the safe side. My hat was on the hat rack so there was no problem."

Jake laughed. "The office must have looked like a tomb with no one there."

"Hoover thought so. He said it looked like an abandoned warehouse and ordered the SAC to find new office space. The FBI soon moved to the GSA building on South Clark Street."

CHAPTER 41
Gerry Patrick Hemming

Jake asked, "Have you ever heard of a man named Hemming? Gerry Patrick Hemming?"

"I can't place him right off hand, but the name sounds vaguely familiar." I knew about Hemming but I wanted to hear what Jake had to say. A confidential source had advised that E. Howard Hunt was in Dallas on November 21, 1963, and had given an envelope of cash to Francisco Fiorini, Aka. Frank Sturgis of Watergate fame, and Gerry Patrick Hemming, just after Sturgis and Hemming smuggled guns into Dallas from Florida. Another source quoted Frank Sturgis as saying, 'We did a really big one in Dallas. We killed the President.' "

Jake said, "Hemming is a big, tall guy. A real soldier of fortune. He does work for the CIA, but is not actually a government employee, as I understand it. He heads up a wild group called the Intercontinental Penetration Force, Interpen for short. He's like Lee Marvin in the movie 'The Dirty Dozen.' He pitched a bunch of the oil guys for some big bucks at the Texas Club in Dallas one day so Interpen could go kill Castro. Some guy in the audience shouted, 'Why don't you go after the big guy?' Someone else shouted, 'Who's that?' Somebody else shouted, 'Smiling Jack,' referring to Jack Kennedy."

"Do you know Hemming?"

"I met him. He's about an inch taller than I am, six feet six I guess. He was in the Marines with Oswald."

"Did Hemming like Kennedy?"

Jake laughed and said, "Hell, no. Hemming hated Kennedy more than Sam Giancana hated Kennedy. If Hemming had some back up he'd have popped Jack himself."

"Do you think he did?"

"He could have been around Dealey Plaza that day."

"But you can't prove it?"

Jake replied, "No, but I wish I could."

"Can you prove anyone was at Dealey Plaza to shoot Kennedy on November 22, 1963?"

"No. Just what I've been told and what I have read in the papers."

I said to Jake, "Then you really don't know who killed Kennedy, other than Oswald? You can't prove in a court of law that anyone else but Oswald took a shot at Kennedy?"

Jake said, "No, just what I've been told. I think some CIA agents like E. Howard Hunt hired people to bring guns to Dallas for the Mafia and the Cubans to use to kill Kennedy. I was told that Hunt took money from some Texas oilmen to pay the assassins. Oswald was just a patsy and that is why he was killed by Jack Ruby."

I asked Jake, "Can you tell me who the oilmen were that gave money to E. Howard Hunt to pay the assassins?"

Jake said, "A friend told me that H.L. Hunt and Clint Murchison, Sr. had given cash to the CIA to get rid of Kennedy."

"Can you name your friend?"

Jake looked up at the ceiling and then said, "No, I can't. He made me promise never to tell anyone for fear of his life. He's too close to Hunt and Murchison."

I said rather sarcastically, "As far as I know all the oilmen that you have mentioned are dead. Hunt, Murchison, Sr., de

Mohrenschildt. The FBI types like Hoover and Tolson are dead. Mafia guys like Giancana, Roselli and Ruby are dead. LBJ is dead. The only CIA types still alive are Frank Sturgis, and Gerry Hemming. Do you know a Billy Byars?"

"Yes. Billy and his wife are oil folks from Tyler, about a hundred miles east of Dallas. They were good friends of Johnson and have attended parties at LBJ's ranch along with Hoover and Tolson. Billy Byars was also thick with Clint Murchison and had attended parties at Del Mar. To respond to your earlier comment, you are forgetting that E. Howard Hunt is still alive."

I nodded. "You are right. I stand corrected." Then I asked, "Do you think Byars may have helped the CIA?"

"I don't know. Billy did whatever LBJ or Murchison asked."

"Why do you think George de Mohrenschildt was shot?"

"Because he knew that Oswald was working with the CIA, Jack Ruby, Giancana, and Roselli in a conspiracy to kill Kennedy. The House Assassinations Committee wanted to question George. In March of 1977, House investigator Gaeton Fonzi went to George's daughter's house but no one answered the door so Fonzi left his business card. The next day George was found dead, shot with a shotgun. The police called the shooting strange but the coroner called it suicide. George and his wife had been writing a book about Oswald and the Kennedy assassination. It was going to be called *I'm a Patsy*. Does suicide sound like something George would have done?"

I replied emphatically, "Not if he and his wife were writing a book about Kennedy's assassination!"

Jake was adamant, "George did not kill himself. The CIA killed him."

"It sounds possible."

Jake said, "George de Mohrenschildt told me in confidence that E. Howard Hunt was the CIA agent who organized and paid for the hit men to kill Kennedy."

I asked, "Are you positive?"

"Yes."

"Did George say who else was involved?"

"George named several guys. Giancana, Trafficante, Marcello, Roselli, Richard Cain, Morales, Hemming, Ferrie, Oswald, Guy Bannister, and Ruby."

"Did George know what they were to do?"

"No, he just said that they were all in a plan to get Kennedy. George didn't give me a blueprint."

"I wish George had given you more."

Jake finally smiled. "Well, Oswald was to be a distraction. I hope you are not mad at me for dragging you all the way from Los Angeles to hear what I had to say?"

"No, not at all. Our talk was very enlightening. I had other things to do in Dallas, so this was just a little side trip." I looked at my watch. It was 5 p.m. "Besides, now I can go back to Dallas and get a Cutty Sark Scotch and a Texas filet mignon."

Jake was relaxed as he walked me to the car. When we shook hands, I said, "I hope your research goes well. I don't plan to say anything to anyone about what you told me here today. There have been too many people killed over the Kennedy assassination. No amount of money can erase the horror of it all."

As I drove away from Jake's home, I had the feeling that Jake may have known more, but it was mostly hearsay, which would not hold up in a court of law. He had been close to the Texas oilmen for 50 years.

As much as I wanted to solve the Kennedy assassination, I knew the feeling of losing a source of information when the wife of a Cuban exile gave me photographs that her husband had taken of Soviet ships in Havana Harbor and I turned them over to the CIA. Her husband was caught and murdered trying to help the United States. I felt that the CIA was behind the death of my source. I was now retired from the FBI and I was not about to get another source into the position where he could be murdered whether that person was Jake Lode or Jake's friend. The government had already murdered some 50 witnesses in an attempt to keep the Kennedy assassination a secret. As Jack Ruby said, "If the truth be known, it's the most amazing story you could ever imagine."

CHAPTER 42
JFK and the Dead Witnesses

I n 1956, I was told by a former CIA agent, who had joined the FBI and with whom I worked on Chicago's Infiltration Squad (S-1), that the CIA had obtained certain chemicals from a university professor of chemistry in Illinois. These chemicals could induce a heart attack and when an autopsy is done on a corpse the chemical will have vanished without a trace. In such cases the Coroner's verdict is always death by heart attack. This FBI agent also told me that the CIA has chemicals which, when injected into the body, cause a reaction of accelerated cancer. When an autopsy is done on a corpse there is no trace of any foul play and the death by cancer is regularly ruled as a natural cause.

Following are some of the approximately 150 individuals who were associated with or who had closer than normal relations with the Kennedy assassination. Some of the deceased, who died unexpectedly, claimed to have had knowledge of a CIA conspiracy. Most of the individuals listed were shot to death. Several hit men, quite possibly E. Howard Hunt's assassins, were terribly busy.

Those individuals listed below obviously had an unusual connection to Kennedy's assassination. The more than 100 individuals who had some association to the Kennedy assassination but who may have died routinely are not listed. Names not listed below can be found in other sources such as the book by Craig Roberts *THE DEAD* WITNESSES; which has an excellent biography on each of the deceased. The book *CROSSFIRE* by Jim Marrs is good. The Internet has additional names with some background description.

I have also listed names that none of the above three sources know about and I have marked them with an asterisk.

Lee Harvey Oswald

November 24, 1963

Oswald allegedly killed JFK. Oswald was shot to death two days later by Jack Ruby, a former member of the Chicago Mob.

Karyn Kupcinet

November 28, 1963

The daughter of Chicago's reporter and talk show host Irv Kupcinet. Karyn was a Hollywood actress. She reportedly told friends that she knew Kennedy was going to be killed. Her strangled body was found in Hollywood on November 30, 1963.

Captain Michael Groves

December 3, 1963

Capt. Michael Groves was an honor guard for JFK's funeral. He reportedly had been practicing burial procedures for three days before Kennedy was killed. Groves was believed to have been poisoned. He was 27.

Jack Zangretti

December, 1963

Zangretti reportedly told friends that Jack Ruby was going to kill Lee Harvey Oswald. Zangretti owned a mob-run gambling resort in Lake Lugert, Oklahoma. Zangretti's bullet ridden body was found floating in Lake Lugert.

Dallas Police Officer J.D. Tippit

November 22, 1963

Officer Tippit was shot to death just after JFK's

assassination. The shooting was witnessed by Domingo Benevides. The shot was heard by Warren Reynolds.

Eddy Benavides

February, 1964

Eddy Benavides was a look-alike brother to officer Tippit's shooting witness, Domingo Benavides. Eddy was shot in the head.

Warren Reynolds

January, 1964

Reynolds heard the shots that killed officer Tippit. He gave chase to a man he saw carrying a pistol and running from the scene but he lost the perpetrator. Reynolds was later shot, but he did not die. Reynolds made a report to the FBI. The FBI told Reynolds they do not investigate attempted murder.

Betty Mooney McDonald

February 13, 1964

Betty McDonald, a Jack Ruby stripper, was found hanged in jail. Her death was considered a suicide.

Bill Chesher

March, 1964

Chesher reportedly had information linking Oswald to Jack Ruby. Before he could tell authorities what he knew he supposedly died of a heart attack

Thomas Henry Killam

March 17, 1964

Thomas Killam, husband of Ruby stripper Wanda Joyce Killam, had fled Dallas in an attempt to avoid being murdered for what he knew about Jack Ruby's involvement in the Kennedy assassination. Killam's body was found in Florida with a slashed throat. Killam had reportedly thrown himself through a plate glass window in an effort to commit suicide.

The authorities want us to believe that Killam committed suicide to avoid being murdered. Is this brilliant, or what?

Bill Hunter

April 24, 1964

Bill Hunter had interviewed Jack Ruby and had met with Ruby's attorney in Ruby's apartment after Ruby killed Oswald. Hunter was an award-winning journalist with the Long Beach Press Telegram in Long Beach, California. Hunter was shot to death at the Long Beach Police Department. Hunter's death was ruled an accident. An officer supposedly dropped his weapon in the Press Room and it discharged when hitting the floor sending a bullet through Hunter's heart. Hunter's death was ruled an unfortunate accident. Will someone please tell me what a police officer was doing playing with his piece in the Long Beach Police Department Press Room?

As for my own personal experience with handguns, I handled my .38 Colt service revolver every day for over 25 years. Not once did I drop it. Not once did I drop it while cleaning it at least once a month after firearms training. Not once have I heard of another agent dropping his service revolver. Not once have I heard of a weapon being dropped accidentally by any police officer except in the case of Bill Hunter where Hunter was shot through the heart. I do not believe for a nano second that Hunter's death was an accident.

Maurice Brooks Gatlin, Sr.

May, 1964

Maurice Gatlin, Sr. was a bag-man and an asset for the CIA. He had worked for former FBI agent Guy Bannister in New Orleans. Authorities want us to believe that before Gatlin could testify before the Warren Commission he had apparently slipped on a banana peel in a Panama City, Florida, hotel and had accidentally fallen from a sixth floor open window causing his death.

John Garret Underhill
May 8, 1964

John Garret Underhill was a CIA agent who had told friends that the CIA was behind the JFK assassination. Before Underhill could testify before a tribunal or commission, his body was found on his bed with a bullet wound behind his left ear and a gun on his left side. The coroner had ruled Underhill's death a suicide. It seems strange to me that a right-handed person would shoot himself behind the left ear. The FBI normally does not investigate suicide; however, since Underhill was a federal officer and the killing of a federal officer is a federal offense the FBI should have investigated Underhill's death.

Hugh Ward
May 23, 1964

Hugh Ward was a private investigator working with Guy Bannister. He died in a plane crash in Mexico along with Delesseps Morrison, Mayor of New Orleans. The plane's pilot was an experienced pilot. The twin-engine Piper Aztec with plenty of fuel ran into trouble on a clear day. Both engines quit at the same time and the plane crashed killing all on board. Authorities want us to believe this happens regularly in small twin-engine private planes on a clear day with plenty of fuel.

Guy F. Bannister, Jr.
June, 1964

Bannister retired under protest from the FBI as SAC of the Chicago Division in 1954. Bannister soon became the Chief of Police in New Orleans until he ran into a problem and was fired. He reportedly knew Lee Harvey Oswald when Oswald worked with the Fair Play for Cuba Committee in New Orleans. Bannister reportedly worked with the CIA and

Bannister knew Clay Shaw and Davis Ferrie, whom District Attorney Jim Garrison had connected to the Kennedy assassination. Jack Martin, Bannister's employee, reported to the FBI that Bannister was involved with the CIA in Kennedy's assassination. The FBI thought Martin was unreliable and so the FBI apparently did nothing. Bannister died of an alleged "heart attack."

My informant Ramon had told me in 1962 that Guy Bannister was working with the CIA, the Chicago Mob, and a patsy from New Orleans, possibly Oswald, in a plan to assassinate President John F. Kennedy at some future location which had not been determined as of October 1962.

Teresa Norton
August, 1964
Norton had been a Ruby employee. She was found shot to death.

James F. Koethe
September 21, 1964
Koethe was a reporter for the *Dallas Times-Herald* and had met with reporter Bill Hunter of the Long Beach, CA. *Press Telegram*, in Ruby's apartment after Ruby killed Oswald. Hunter was "accidentally" shot through the heart, but Jim Koethe was murdered with a fatal martial arts chop to the throat. Certainly Koethe did not render a fatal chop to his own throat. Why would two reporters from two different cities, who had met in Ruby's apartment, die within five months of each other? Apparently authorities want us to believe this is a normal event in the United States.

It is my opinion that Hunter and Koethe were murdered to keep them quiet. It is also my opinion that J. Edgar Hoover, W. Mark Felt, James H. Gale and other top FBI officials covered up these murders in an act of treason to protect the

CIA, the Chicago Mob, certain FBI informants and the FBI's mishandling of the Oswald investigation prior to Kennedy's assassination.

Mary Pinchot

October, 1964

Pinchot was a close friend of John Kennedy. She had reportedly replaced Judy Campbell as Kennedy's pillowing partner after Hoover confronted Kennedy about sleeping with Judy Campbell. Pinchot kept a diary, which the CIA is believed to have seized after finding her dead body. The cause of death was ruled as murder. Pinchot was shot to death while out jogging. I'm surprised authorities did not say she had run into a school of speeding bullets.

Dorothy Kilgallen

November 8, 1965

Kilgallen, a nationally known syndicated newspaper columnist, had interviewed Jack Ruby in the judge's chambers at the time of Ruby's trial. Kilgallen was reportedly going to blow the lid off of the Kennedy assassination. She allegedly died from an overdose of alcohol. Her notes were reportedly given to Mrs. Earl E.T. Smith who died just three days later.

Mrs. Earl E.T Smith

November 11, 1965

Mrs. Smith, who was also a columnist and who wrote under the name of "Miss Florence Pritchet," died from a cerebral hemorrhage just three days following the untimely death of Dorothy Kilgallen. Could Mrs. Smith have died because the CIA thought she could have exposed the conspiracy to murder President Kennedy? We will never know. The FBI wants us to believe this is just another natural death.

Lieutenant Commander William Bruce Pitzer USN

October 29, 1966

Lt. Cmdr. Pitzer was the x-ray technician who filmed Kennedy's autopsy. Pitzer reportedly told friends that his experience with the Kennedy autopsy was horrifying. Pitzer planned to retire and take a new job at $45,000.00 a year. Instead, he allegedly committed suicide by shooting himself in the head.

Jack Ruby

January, 3, 1967

Jack Ruby was tied to the Chicago Mafia and reportedly ran guns. While Ruby was in jail for shooting Oswald, he complained of a strange visitor who injected him with an unknown substance. Ruby's complaints were ignored. Ruby wanted to testify before the Warren Commission but the Commission refused to hear his testimony. Jack Ruby's murder conviction was overturned, but while he was awaiting a new trial he died of lung cancer.

David William Ferrie

February 22, 1967

Ferrie was associated with Guy Bannister, Lee Harvey Oswald and gun running. Ferrie was known to have been involved with the CIA in the Kennedy assassination. Ferrie considered himself to be a hypnotist. Jack Martin, Bannister's employee, told the FBI that Ferrie had hypnotized Lee Harvey Oswald into shooting Kennedy. Ferrie was reportedly connected to the getaway team, which was to fly co-conspirators out of Dallas to freedom. Within a week of Jim Garrison releasing Ferrie's name to the public as having a connection to the Kennedy assassination and being a potential witness, Ferrie was found dead with a brain hemorrhage. His death was ruled a suicide.

The FBI did not follow up on Martin's information because they thought Martin was unreliable. The FBI claims that it does not judge the information it receives, or render a decision, but here is a clear case of the FBI receiving and judging information and not acting upon Martin's information. This is a clear act of treason.

Eladio Del Valle

February 22, 1967

My informant Ramon was a good friend of Eladio Del Valle. It is quite possible that Ramon obtained much of his information about the planned Kennedy assassination from Eladio. It should be noted that one of Eladio's friends, David Ferrie, also died on February 22, 1967, which was ruled a suicide. Eladio did not fare as well as David Ferrie. Eladio was reportedly shot to death.

The FBI wants us to believe that Eladio and Ferrie committed suicide on the same day?

Jimmy Hoffa

July, 1972

Long time Teamster boss Jimmy Hoffa reportedly sent a message to Carlos Marcello and Santo Trafficante in 1963, that Kennedy had to be killed. Hoffa went missing in July of 1972 and his body has never been found.

*Richard Cain

December 20, 1973

Richard Cain originally was a Chicago cop and a bagman for Sam Giancana. Cain became a trainer at the CIA's JM/Wave training camp in Florida and a top FBI informant. FBI agent Bill Roemer considered Cain to be a Special Agent of the FBI as well as did Bureau supervisor Marshall Rutland. Cain was reportedly involved in Kennedy's assassination and two reliable sources told me that Cain was present on the Grassy Knoll when Kennedy was assassinated. Cain was shot to death at a restaurant in typical Chicago gangland style.

Sam Giancana

June 19, 1975

Giancana was shot to death in his own home before he had a chance to testify before the Senate Intelligence Committee. Giancana was trained at the CIA's JM/Wave camp in Florida. Bill Roemer refused to believe that one of his pocket informants Dominic "Butch" Blasi, Giancana's bodyguard, had been involved in the shooting death of Sam Giancana.

*FBI agent Marshall "Maz" Rutland

December 13, 1975

FBI agent Maz Rutland worked on the Top Hoodlum Program in Chicago. He conducted several interviews of females associated with Mob figures in _my_ Chicago apartment. Rutland later became a supervisor of Organized Crime at FBI headquarters. Rutland was a physical fitness buff. Rutland died of supposedly natural causes at the age of 46. There was no autopsy.

Johnny Roselli

August, 1976

Chicago Mob figure and a trainee at the CIA's JM/Wave camp in Florida, was found stuffed in an oil drum in Dumbfounding Bay near Miami, Florida. Roselli had been scheduled to testify before the Senate Intelligence Committee.

FBI agent William C. Sullivan

July 16, 1978

William C. Sullivan was Hoover's number three man in charge of the FBI's Intelligence Division. Hoover gave Sullivan orders to issue something indicating that Lee Harvey Oswald was the lone assassin of President Kennedy. Sullivan was reportedly "accidentally" shot to death in a hunting accident. Sullivan had reportedly been mistaken for a deer while wearing a bright orange jacket.

I have seen many deer in the wild, but I have never seen one wearing a bright orange jacket.

David Sanchez Morales, aka "Indio"

1978

Morales, a former CIA agent, was building a retirement home in Arizona in 1978, when he made a public outburst at a gathering of friends. Morales had been talking about JFK. He said, after having had several drinks, "We took care of that son of a bitch, didn't we?"

Morales died of a "heart attack" at age 52.

*Joseph M. Culkin

March 16, 1982

An agent I used to work with in Chicago when Culkin was our supervisor advised me after I had retired that Culkin was alone in a car accident. My friend did not have any details. Culkin died at the age of 56.

*FBI agent Ralph Hill

1985

FBI agent Ralph Hill worked on the THP squad in Chicago. He was the case agent on Sam Giancana. Hill interviewed girl friends of Chicago Mob bosses in my apartment. Hill also interviewed Judy Campbell, a friend of President Kennedy. Hill also supervised the THP squad in Miami, Florida. While ASAC in Milwaukee, Wisconsin, Ralph Hill reportedly suffered a massive heart attack in 1976 at the age of 48, but he did not die until 1985. Hill died at age 57.

Hill knew about the CIA's plan to kill Kennedy because I had told him in 1962.

It seems strange that the two agents who interviewed girlfriends of mafia bosses in my apartment and who supervised the FBI's Top Hoodlum Programs and my Chicago supervisor died at such early ages. Rutland died at age 46 and Hill almost died at age 48. Culkin died at age 56 and Sullivan was shot to death. This is not a coincidence folks.

*FBI agent Will H. Griffin

August, 1982

Griffin reportedly claimed publicly that Oswald was definitely an FBI informant. However, it has been reported in the 1996 book, "Assignment Oswald," by ex-FBI agent James P. Hosty, Jr. that all Dallas agents were required to sign an affidavit that Oswald was not an FBI informant. Griffin's cause of death was reported as cancer. James P. Hosty, Jr. signed an affidavit and he is still alive and well.

It should be noted that the FBI covered up the fact that Julius Carl Butler was a documented informant for the FBI with an extensive file for several years. Butler perjured himself in court, the FBI lied in court and Geronimo Pratt spent 25 years in prison, so I don't put much stock in what the FBI or James P. Hosty, Jr. says about Oswald not being an informant, if not for the FBI then certainly for the CIA. If Oswald was not an informant, and if Hosty never met Oswald, why would Hosty go interview Oswald after President Kennedy had been assassinated?

Frank Sturgis

December 4, 1993

Sturgis was linked to the Kennedy assassination as having transported weapons to Dallas the day before Kennedy was assassinated. Sturgis was arrested in 1972 during the Watergate break-in and was sent to prison. Sturgis reportedly died of cancer.

CHAPTER 43
Craig Roberts on Dealey Plaza

In his book *KILL ZONE, A Sniper Looks at Dealey Plaza;* Craig Roberts presents a convincing argument that a French Connection was involved in the assassination of President Kennedy.

By 1961, Attorney General Bobby Kennedy had established an all out assault against New Orleans mob boss Carlos Marcello. In return Marcello decided to order a hit on Bobby's brother. It has been speculated that Marcello turned to Santos Trafficante, the big Mafia boss in Miami. This may have been done for three reasons. Marcello needed help with such a huge undertaking. The second reason was that Hoover's G-Men would surely dig up any evidence against Marcello if he used his usual suspects to whack the president. The third reason may have been the fact that the FBI in Miami did not know squat about the Italian Mafia, according to Bill Roemer and Ralph Hill.

It appears logical that Marcello would have asked his good friend, Santos Trafficante, the Miami boss who had connections overseas, to bring in someone like Lucien Sarti. It has been speculated that Trafficante used his Corsican Mafia connections to hire foreign hit men in an effort to dispel attention away from the U.S. Mafia.

Craig Roberts writes that a reporter named Steve J. Rivele, a Los Angeles reporter and writer, discovered material that the Corsican Brotherhood provided the out-of-the country hit team for the American Mafia. These men were Sauveur Pironti, Jorge Bocognini, and Lucien Sarti. They reportedly traveled from Marseille to Mexico City and hooked up with their counterparts from the CIA's ZR/RIFLE team.

Both Roemer and Ralph Hill told me that Sam Giancana and Richard Cain had been in Mexico taking care of business.

Craig Roberts writes that the Corsican guys had crossed over into the U.S. and were met by the American Mafia out of Chicago, Sam Giancana's people, and driven to Dallas.

I do not dispute what Craig Roberts has written. I believe that with the information furnished to me by a very reliable source, which has been corroborated by a second very reliable source, it reveals quite possibly that both Cain and Sarti were on the grassy knoll at the time President Kennedy was shot. However, my two sources advised in 2004 that Richard Cain was dressed in a dark suit and tie and wearing horn-rimmed glasses.

Sarti was known for dressing as a police officer when committing acts of assassination.

It makes more sense that two professional assassins were on the grassy knoll overseeing the hit on Kennedy than to think, as the Warren Commission did, that Kennedy was killed by a single magic bullet fired from a cheap mail-order rifle from a position in the book store by Lee Harvey Oswald.

Craig Roberts is an expert sniper having been trained by the U.S. Marine Corps. Craig Roberts has authored the books *ONE SHOT—ONE KILL; America's Combat Snipers (Pocket Books, 1990); POLICE SNIPER* (Pocket Books, 1993), and *KILL ZONE A Sniper Looks at Dealey Plaza, (Typhoon Press, 1994).*

I think Craig Roberts is a better judge as to what actually happened at Dealey Plaza, based on the forensic evidence and the witness reports, than a group of half-baked politicians who had an agenda to cover up the CIA's plot to kill the President. It is not that I can't accept the possibility that President Kennedy was killed by a single man. I know for a fact that there was an ongoing conspiracy to kill Kennedy because Ramon had told me that such was the case in 1962. Although much of the evidence was covered up or distorted, the murders of so many witnesses have to be a clue that Oswald was not alone. An overt act by one person in a conspiracy is sufficient to establish the element that a conspiracy did occur.

CHAPTER 44
Dealey Plaza, Dallas, Texas 1999

It was Saturday, November 20, 1999, and a beautiful sunny day in Dallas. Craig Roberts and I walked around Dealey Plaza, which had become the crime scene of the twentieth century. We viewed this historic place, not from the eyes of the many gawking tourists, but as retired investigators who were experts in the field of law enforcement.

Craig Roberts, author of *KILL ZONE, A Sniper Looks At Dealey Plaza,* accompanied me to Dealey Plaza in Dallas, Texas. It was my first walk through the area, but Craig's first visit prompted him to write the objective book on President Kennedy's murder. We parked in the lot behind the grassy knoll. Craig, a former US Marine Corps Vietnam sniper, explained the area and what he thought had happened on November 22, 1963. I quietly observed the crime scene as Craig's narration of events took me back to that fateful day that shocked the world. The image of President Kennedy being shot in the face haunted me still. We stood where one of the fatal shots most likely had been fired.

Craig said, "One sniper shot from behind the fence here where witnesses had reported they heard shots. Another witness, a military man on leave taking pictures to show his buddies back at the base, reported that after shots were fired a man dressed in a Dallas police uniform came from behind the fence and grabbed his camera and ripped out the film. The bogus police officer then headed back to the parking lot and out of sight."

I was reminded of my early days in the FBI's Training School where we new agents had been taught to use the 30.06 Springfield rifle. Shooting a rifle at paper targets one hundred and two hundred yards came easy for me. As a kid I had a lot of practice with the Daisy Red Ryder B-B Gun. Because the Daisy B-B Gun had no recoil I had not developed a reflex action to the Springfield rifle, as had other new agents. As a result I won the rifle match of the New Agent's class. I had scored higher than the next highest scorer in class who had been one of the western state champions who scored a 95. The FBI did not train snipers in 1951, but if they had I surely would have been one of their top snipers with a score of 97 out of 100 using adjustable iron sights. Prior to entering the FBI I received firearms training in the US Navy and scored a 19 out of a possible 21 bull's eyes. The Navy Instructor asked me, "Where in the hell did you learn to shoot like that?" I had the highest score in my company with the standard military issue .45 automatic.

I said to Craig, "Bogus police officer? I read somewhere that a man in a police uniform was in this lot on the day of the shooting?"

"Yes, but the Dallas police have no record of a uniformed officer being assigned to this spot on the day of the assassination."

I asked, "What clown would wear a police uniform to observe Kennedy unless he had had an evil motive?"

Craig stepped to a spot behind the fence and said, "I believe that a French Corsican Mafia hit man named Lucien Sarti, wearing a police uniform, which was one of his trademarks, made the head shot from behind this fence." Craig assumed the position of a sniper, and squeezed off a shot. "Pow! That is the shot that threw Kennedy's head back, as shown in the Zapruder film."

It is noted that Abraham Zapruder, an amateur photographer, stood on a monument retaining wall and filmed Kennedy's motorcade as it drove by the Grassy Knoll. A few frames show that Kennedy was shot from the front and that his head literally exploded like the melon in the 1973 movie "Day of the Jackal," directed by Fred Zinneman and starring Edward Fox. The Zapruder film caught the entire sequence of events surrounding JFK's assassination and the film is irrefutable evidence that Lee Harvey Oswald could _not_ have been the lone assassin.

In 2004, two different reliable sources advised me that they had been told by a relative of Richard Cain that Cain was on the Grassy Knoll when Kennedy was shot. One of the reliable sources was acquainted with the family of the former Chicago Mob boss Tony Accardo.

I asked Craig, "Is that the film Zapruder's family recently sold for sixteen million bucks?"

It is noted that the *Los Angeles Times* reported in August 1999, that the heirs of Abraham Zapruder sold the notorious assassination film to the National Archives for $16 million.

"Right."

"Wasn't Sarti that OAS French assassin?" Ramon had told me that Richard Cain was involved in the assassination plot, but I did not know then that Cain was reportedly one of the men on the grassy knoll. I did not mention anything to Roberts because I wanted to hear what he had to say about the shooting. Plus, I did not know until 2004 that Richard Cain was actually on the Grassy Knoll.

"Yes. It was his modus operandi to wear either a soldier's uniform or a police uniform during an assassination attempt. Sarti was the 'Jackal' who attempted to assassinate former French President Charles de Gaulle."

"I saw the movie version, where the Jackal was shown as an Englishman in the original "Day of The Jackal."

Craig explained what he thought had happened. "The head shot was most likely made with mercury filled hollow point, another Sarti trademark. The autopsy showed spots of what could be mercury on Kennedy's skull, but this was not brought out by the Warren Commission."

"I remember seeing the Zapruder film where Kennedy's head went back. That is where our illustrious FBI Director, J. Edgar Hoover, claimed the driver of the limo had accelerated causing Kennedy's head to go backwards."

Craig shook his head and said, "No. Kennedy was shot before the limo sped up. The Secret Service agent, who had been walking behind the car, said Kennedy was shot first and then the agent jumped aboard the limo as it accelerated."

"When I saw replays of the shooting on TV, I knew immediately that Hoover was lying when he declared that Oswald was the lone assassin. You can see the Secret Service agent jogging behind the car. The movement of Kennedy's head going backwards from an alleged shot to the back of the head was against everything they taught us on gunshot wounds at the FBI's National Academy," I said.

"And totally inconsistent with all the shots I saw in Vietnam," said Craig.

I asked, "Where is the sewer?"

Craig motioned down the hill, "It's over there."

CHAPTER 45
Johnny Roselli in the Sewer

I said to Craig, as we walked down the hill to the sewer drain, "I'm anxious to see the drain hole because I had been told by a reliable Mafia source that Johnny Roselli shot at Kennedy from the sewer. I have trouble visualizing Roselli crawling around in some sewer." I laughed, "Of course when a Mafia boss like Giancana or Trafficante orders you to crawl into a sewer you crawl into a sewer, or else." I laughed again and said, "It's an offer you can't refuse."

Craig pointed to the center lane of Elm Street, "See that X? That's where Kennedy was shot."

The distance took me by surprise. I said, "That's a long way from the Book Depository!"

"Exactly! It is eighty-eight yards. Kennedy's limousine went North on Houston Street toward the Book Depository, passing the jail and the Records Building, just south of the Dal-Tex building. The Lincoln convertible slowed almost to a stop, turned left at the intersection of Houston and Elm streets, and passed in front of the Book Depository. It then proceeded down Elm in the center lane to this spot, where the head shot occurred."

I remembered that the Dal-Tex building was reportedly owned by the father of then CIA agent E. Howard Hunt. The CIA agent reportedly had offices on the sixth floor of the Dal-Tex building. The roof of the building was an excellent place to call the shots at JFK and to make the first shot which could have been the signal for Oswald and others to fire at will.

I listened to Craig explain the route of the limo. Then I asked, "Why didn't Oswald shoot Kennedy at the intersection of Houston and Elm instead of down here? His target was approaching one hundred yards and going away. That's stupid."

"Because Oswald did not shoot anyone. He was downstairs at the second floor break room. Someone else waited until Kennedy reached the kill zone where the other shooters were to open fire from all sides. The shots from the eastern sixth floor window were diversionary, to pin the blame on Oswald."

"That makes sense. If Oswald was the lone killer he would have taken his best shot at close range when the limo almost stopped. It isn't logical, if Oswald was a lone nut killer as the Warren Commission said, to wait until Kennedy is going away when the distance is increasing. An assassin would have nailed Kennedy at the intersection when he was almost directly below. It would have been like shooting fish in a barrel at the intersection."

"Exactly."

"What's the distance from the sixth floor to the intersection?"

"About thirty-five yards."

"Thirty-five yards? Hell, I could have emptied my old six shot .38 Colt Service Revolver into Kennedy's head in less than five seconds. With a sniper's rifle I could have popped his eyeball or put one in Kennedy's ear. As a teenager, I once shot a rabbit in the ear with a B-B gun from the third story window of the family house, which is about half the distance we are talking about to the intersection. Or, with a Remington model 870 shotgun and a load of rifle slugs I could have chopped

Kennedy's head off right there at the intersection, with one or two shots." I became irritated. "There is no way in hell that Oswald was the lone shooter! Oswald was a patsy! It was a setup! It was theatrics at its best while the real killers went to work at the kill zone and then vanished among the hysterical tourists! Hoover's lone nut theory is total fiction!" I remembered what Ramon had said but I said nothing to Roberts. I was not prepared to tell him all of what I knew.

Craig continued after I vented my emotions. "The shot that hit Governor Connally came from the west end of the Book Depository—possibly from the sixth floor window, but not the 'Sniper's Nest.' There were photo studies done and two figures could be seen in that window."

I laughed, "The Warren Commission certainly covered that up nicely."

"The throat shot was from the area of the Grassy Knoll." Craig continued, "As was the head shot, although the head shot could have come from the sewer, but since the skull was altered between Parkland Hospital in Dallas and the Naval Medical Center in Bethesda, Maryland, we'll never know. The throat shot was probably fired by a Winchester .22 model 74 bolt action with a silencer."

"Is that the one you mentioned in your book? My Cuban source said the CIA had special rifles made with no identifying marks on them."

Craig said, "Yes. This is the old OSS sentry take out rifle and it is still used by the CIA. And no one heard the shot that hit Kennedy in the throat, which was the first wound in the sequence of events."

I stood at the sewer and aimed my finger at the X, simulating a head shot. To me, making a head shot from the sewer at a man sitting on the right side of a convertible coming head on looked like a piece of cake. I said, "A Cuban exile, who trained with Johnny Roselli in Florida, claimed in 1961 that the CIA taught them techniques with rifles that were made especially for the CIA for assassination. The CIA wanted Roselli and the Cubans to kill Castro. Could Roselli have used a Winchester .22 model 74 bolt action here in the sewer?"

"It's possible."

I said, "Roselli was known to use a .22 in Chicago. In fact a .22 is preferred by Mafia hit men."

"They use a .22 when a clean hit is needed," answered Craig.

I said, "A high ranking Mafia source told me after I retired and blew the whistle on the FBI's wrongdoing in my book, *FBI SECRETS,* that Johnny Roselli was the sewer man who shot JFK. My friend said Roselli was pissed off because Giancana didn't send anyone around to pick him up at the other end of the sewer after he shot Kennedy. Roselli originally gave columnist Jack Anderson a song and dance routine that the communists did it. Roselli thought Hoover would go for the communist gig. What Anderson didn't know was that Roselli was jerking Anderson's chain. We believed there was no love lost between Giancana and Roselli. Maybe Sam set him up. The usual weapon for a mob hit was a High-Standard Duromatic with a silencer, a small-caliber, lightweight .22."

I thought about the different shots that Craig had explained and the alleged shot from the sixth floor window of the Book Depository. The timing was important. I asked Craig, "When did the throat shot occur?"

"According to the Zapruder film Kennedy was holding his throat when the limo came into view from behind the Stemmons Freeway sign, which is no longer here. That was probably the first shot. It was probably intended to hit Kennedy in the head, but the shooter had too much of a lead, or the shooter's elevation was off."

"I had to laugh when I saw your replica of Oswald's 6.5 mm Mannlicher-Carcano that you brought to the Lancer conference. After training with the FBI's top grade weapons, the Carcano looked to be homemade. And that offset scope. What a joke! I examined the Carcano and there is no way Oswald could have fired three shots in 5.6 seconds, with or without using the scope, and aim at a small moving target."

Craig asked, "How did you like my demonstration to kick off the conference on Friday?"

"Without firing a shot you proved Oswald could not have done what J. Edgar Hoover, the Warren Commission, and the House Select Committee on Assassinations claimed he had done."

"Oswald could not have used the scope," Craig added.

"I know. I looked through the scope at a car in the parking lot across from the Dallas Grand Hotel and it took three seconds to access the target again after a simulation shot without trying to reload. The scope is offset to the left which means that the view through the scope and the view through the iron sights converge at some point. It is at that exact point that the scope is any good. Any shorter or longer distance from the convergence point and the scope is worthless. The fact that Oswald lobbed one shot into the curb proves he was way off after the first shot."

Craig responded, "And the other shots"

"What other shots?"

"Someone threw a wild shot that splintered on the curb and hit James Tague in the face as he stood near the underpass."

"I'm confused. If Oswald supposedly fired three times and missed twice, how then could Kennedy be hit in the back of the neck once and in the front of the face once? Oswald must have developed a bullet that could make a sharp left turn. Senator Spector is either mentally retarded or lying to cover up what really happened when he dreamed up the single-bullet-theory."

It is noted that Senator Arlen Spector was appointed in 1964 as assistant counsel to the Warren Commission to investigate the assassination of President Kennedy. Spector developed the single-bullet-theory. Spector later used the assassination exposure to become Pennsylvania's senator in 1980. During the President Clinton–Monica Lewinsky scandal, Senator Spector defended special counsel Ken Starr and repeatedly misstated Linda Tripp's name as Linda TRAPP in some sort of Freudian slip. During the senate hearings on the burning of the Branch Davidian compound at Waco, Senator Spector continually misstated the Bureau of Alcohol, Tobacco, and Firearms, ATF as AFT.

Craig said, "The back shot could have come from the roof of the Dal-Tex Building."

"How do you figure that?"

"A few years ago a spent .30-06 sabot cartridge was found on the roof under an air conditioner. It was bright and shiny on one side and tarnished on the other side like it had been there for a long time. Plus, prisoners in the jail overlooking the Dal-Tex building said they saw a man on the roof at the time of the shooting, but the Warren Commission did not interview any of the inmates."

"The inmates could have been some of their best witnesses."

Craig said, "Exactly. Let's go into the Book Depository."

CHAPTER 46
The Sniper's Nest

I said, "Okay." Craig headed toward the west side of the building and then realized the front door had been shifted to the Houston Street side. We walked to the Houston Street entrance and I said, "This looks like a tourist trap."

A special entrance had been built and a toll booth installed on the first floor. The entrance fee was $5 for a senior citizen ticket. We entered through an electronic gate, similar to those in the any airport.

I said, "Someone should tell the museum operator that Kennedy is dead." Craig and I put our car keys in a little basket and walked through the gate without any trouble. We rode a cattle-car size elevator to the sixth floor exhibition room. Craig took me directly to the "Sniper's Nest" passing all the black and white exhibits of Kennedy being shot. News announcements from several sources and from different directions blasted away at the curiosity seekers.

Craig stopped and pointed to the "Sniper's Nest." "This is where Oswald supposedly killed Kennedy. Can you imagine trying to shoot out that window with all those boxes in the way and that water pipe next to the window?"

"Ha! That's a joke. This whole place is disgusting." It was grossly offensive to see that the sixth floor of the Book Depository had been turned into an amusement center of death, with black and white pictures and movies and voice recordings of announcers such as Walter Cronkite announcing the events of what had happened that fateful day on November 22, 1963. The whole exhibit was indecorous. It was especially obnoxious when I considered the fact that someone was making money from John Kennedy's assassination.

Craig took me over to another window where we studied the street below. Craig said, "Kennedy's limo came North on Houston and then turned left onto Elm."

"No left turns."

"What?"

"Hoover visited Dallas in 1959 and he told the agents, 'There will be no left turns.'"

Craig asked, "What was that all about?"

"A few months earlier Hoover and Tolson were doing their annual three week vacation at Hotel Del Charro in Del Mar, California. Neither Hoover nor Tolson ever took "vacations." They were always "on duty" while visiting the race track in California. One day the Director's chauffeur-driven Cadillac limo, while making a left turn, had been hit from behind by another car. Hoover had not been injured but he definitely had been shaken up. After that Hoover instructed his associate director, Clyde Tolson, to sit on the left side, where Hoover usually sat. He told the chauffeur that, 'There will be no left turns.' The Director had been correct, if Kennedy's limo had not made a left turn Kennedy would not have been shot."

"Yeah, sure."

Craig was silent while I studied the two streets below. Elm Street is three lanes wide. I timed pedestrians as they crossed Elm. The average time was about fifteen seconds. An eternity for a sniper. I imagined the limousine coming North on Houston, slowing too almost the speed of a pedestrian crossing the street, and then turning left just below the sixth floor of the Book Depository. I imagined the slowness of the limo as it turned. My finger followed an imaginary curve at Houston and Elm. I imagined taking a shot at Kennedy at the closest possible range, Pow! Possibly thirty-five yards. Pow! The FBI's Practical Pistol Course, using a .38 Colt revolver, started at sixty yards. With a Remington 12 gauge shotgun model 870, with which I had been trained by the FBI, I could have put one rifle slug round, about the size of the average thumb, into Kennedy's face blowing his head open like the melon in the movie "Day of the Jackal."

Neither I nor Oswald would have needed a second shot at thirty-five yards. But hold on, Oswald did not shoot at the closest point. He waited until the distance tripled. Oswald could have had an easy shot at the intersection, but he waited until the water pipe was in his way and the trees were becoming an obstruction. This was not the work of one who wanted Kennedy dead; it was the work of someone who wanted to create a distraction. Oswald was a diversion. Anyone who visits the "Sniper's Nest" can clearly see that Oswald had forfeited his best shot when the limo turned onto Elm Street.

I turned to Craig and said, "Oswald didn't kill Kennedy. He may have shot at him but he didn't kill him."

Craig said, "I kept quiet on purpose to let you study the scene."

"Anyone bent on killing Kennedy would have done it when his car made the left turn—when the target was facing the shooter. A sniper doesn't wait until the target is nearly out of sight to begin shooting. Hoover, the Warren Commission, and the House Select Committee on Assassinations have all taken a leave of their senses."

Craig asked, "Where were you on the day Kennedy was shot?"

"I was in Washington, D.C. It was the last day of In-Service training. I will never forget that day. Inspector Mark Felt came to the classroom and dismissed us early. Felt said the President Kennedy had just been shot."

CHAPTER 47
Ross Gelbspan on Oliver Revell

Ross Gelbspan is a Pulitzer Prize-winning journalist with more than 40 years experience at the *Washington Post, Philadelphia Bulletin, Village Voice* and *Boston Globe,* among others.

Oliver "Buck" Revell once held the number three position in the FBI as Associate Deputy Director.

In his 1991 book, *BREAK-IN, DEATH THREATS AND THE FBI*, published by South End Press, Boston, Gelbspan is extremely critical of Oliver "Buck" Revell. Gelbspan referred to Revell as a liar and as an FBI official who clearly and "systematically uses distortion, disinformation and deliberate lies as official instruments of policy. Whether those lies are directed toward political adversaries, news reporters, other agencies of the executive branch or overseers in Congress charged with monitoring the Bureau's operations, the record of the FBI's counter-terrorism and counter-intelligence units demonstrates unequivocally that it is not to be trusted to tell the truth. With the acquiescence of the Congressional committees, the FBI has succeeded in lying its way out of a series of scandals whose casualties have been truth, the democratic process, and the First Amendment to the Constitution." (Page 227).

Gelbspan's book "raises the curtain on the Bureau's secret attempts to undermine and demonize the nationwide network of individuals and protest groups opposed to the Reagan

Administration's Central America policies and programs. Ross Gelbspan demonstrates that the more than two hundred verified instances of break-ins, burglaries, death threats, harassment, and arson cannot be viewed, as many preferred, as a series of scattered horror stories, but must be recognized as unified by an overall plot to eliminate critics and opponents of Reagan's Central America initiatives." (From the Forward by Frank J. Donner, author of *The Age of Surveillance,* page X).

The main thrust of Gelbspan's book centers around the FBI's attack on the Committee in Solidarity with the People of El Salvador (CISPES), which investigation was concocted to destroy CISPES and silence anyone opposing Reagan's policy in Central America.

"In the spring of 1990, Adm. John Poindexter, the former National Security Adviser to whom Oliver North responded, was sentenced to six months in prison for lying to Congress. At Poindexter's sentencing, U.S. District Judge Harold Greene said that, had Poindexter not served time in jail, 'it would be tantamount to a statement that a scheme to lie to Congress is of no great moment, and that even if the perpetrators are found out, the courts will treat their criminal acts as no more than minor infractions.' Judge Greene held that Poindexter and North had acted 'in violation of a principle fundamental to this constitutional republic—that those elected by and responsible to the people shall make the important policy decisions, and that their decisions may not be nullified by appointed officials who happen to be in positions that give them the ability to operate programs prohibited by law.' " (*Boston Globe,* June 12, 1990. Page 227-228).

"It is perplexing that the appropriate officials of the FBI—Ronald Davenport, Oliver Revell, and William Webster—have not been held to the same standards as Poindexter and other federal employees who have been convicted of lying to Congress. The message inherent in the lack of such convictions is that the very agency empowered to enforce the federal laws of the country is, itself, beyond the reach of those laws." (Page 228).

"Given the Bureau's tenacious adherence to illegal domestic operations in the face of public and Congressional criticism, given its unwillingness or inability to police its own actions in accordance with the requirements of free speech embedded in the Constitution, and given its time-tested proclivity to act, not as a guardian of the law but as a proprietary police force for the incumbent power structure, there seems no reason for advocates of civil liberties to accept, once again, another promise that the FBI will respect the basic rights of freedom and privacy of U.S. citizens." (P 228).

Gelbspan claims that Frank Varelli, who was the FBI's informant or asset in CISPES, knew that the FBI was giving information to the El Salvador National Guard. Gelbspan writes that, "When Revell told Congress the FBI did not trade information, he was absolutely lying. He knew I (Varelli) called the intelligence unit of the Guard day and night." (Page 134 and Gelbspan's interview with Frank Varelli).

FBIHQ teletype to the Milwaukee FBI office dated March 29, 1984, referring to an inquiry by Sen. Robert Kasten of Wisconsin concerning the FBI's interview of one of Kasten's constituent's states, "Milwaukee is not to divulge any information concerning this investigation or acknowledge the existence of this investigation to anyone outside the FBI."

(Page 2 and FBI Document: CISPES Headquarters file 199-8848-Section 6: Number 254).

What are we to believe when Revell writes this? "I certainly wished that I could have found even a scintilla of evidence that the worst political crime in our nation's history was a conspiracy."

It is my opinion from reading Gelbspan's book that Gelbspan has fairly well documented the fact that Oliver Revell is a creator of disinformation.

CHAPTER 48
The FBI's Liar-of-the-Century

W. Mark Felt was an FBI agent from 1942 until his retirement in 1973.

In 2005, Felt became known as "Deep Throat," the man who crept into dark garages, late at night, like a guttersnipe, to leak to Washington Post reporter Bob Woodward confidential FBI information that had been collected by other FBI agents who actually worked on the Watergate case. Felt himself purloined facts developed by field agents and used it as his own private information to pursue a personal vendetta. In my opinion, the purpose of this trashy and tasteless betrayal of a sitting President was to get even with President Richard Nixon because Nixon had not appointed the pompous and portentous W. Mark Felt as the new FBI director after J. Edgar Hoover died in 1972.

I believe this empty suit of a man, full of childish resentment, had managed to bring down a presidency during the war in Vietnam, not the least bit concerned about what affect it would have on world relations. My belief is that this minuscule minded Mark Felt, who for many years had lived a troubled family life, had clawed his way up to the eye of the FBI pyramid. Felt, who had been the head of the FBI Goon Squad, or Inspection Division for many years, where he had control over the lives of thousands of special agents, could not control his own wife and daughter. I was told by my supervisor in Los Angeles, William John Nolan, that Felt's wife was a nervous wreck while living with the status struck inspector and that she had killed herself to escape the horror of the arrogant one. Nolan said that Mark's daughter was living in a religious commune. Felt was the laughing stock of many field agents, especially those in Los Angeles, who knew the inside story, that the all-powerful controller could not control his own family.

Because of what Felt had done to get even with the world for his family problems, Nixon was nearly impeached by Congress based upon information Felt leaked to Bob Woodward of the Washington Post. Nixon saved face and resigned.

It was common knowledge among FBI agents in 1972, at least in Los Angeles, that Mark Felt was "Deep Throat." William John Nolan, the coordinator of the security squads in Los Angeles and my supervisor when I had first arrived in Los Angeles in 1970, told me that Felt was mad as hell because he had not been appointed Director of the FBI and so Felt made it a personal vendetta to get even with Nixon. Many ex-agents who were not in the FBI at the time, such as William Turner, author of *HOOVER'S FBI, the Man and the Myth,* had figured out in a heartbeat the true identity of Deep Throat.

Mark Felt lied to L. Patrick Gray, the acting FBI director, denying that he was Deep Throat. Mark Felt lied in court about being Deep Throat. Mark Felt lied in his book *THE FBI PYRAMID* about being Deep Throat.

Mark Felt has admitted that when his wife killed herself, Mark lied to his own daughter about how her mother had died.

In my opinion, Mark Felt's actions as "Deep Throat" fit his personal character as a habitual liar when he was in the FBI. It was rumored that Mark Felt started his FBI career as a draft dodger. After finishing law school and with WW II underway in Europe it was only a matter of time before Felt would be drafted into the army. So, to avoid being drafted, W. Mark Felt joined the FBI on January 26, 1942, where he would have a permanent draft deferment. This was the beginning of Felt's countless *big lies*. It was rumored that Felt trampled over his fellow agents during his entire career on his way to the top of the FBI pyramid.

Early in his career Felt was soon assigned to Bureau headquarters in Washington, DC, where he reviewed espionage cases. In his own words Felt writes in the book *THE FBI PYRAMID* that "ninety-eight percent of the cases could have been closed immediately." Felt writes that being new to the work and overly cautious he resolved any doubts in favor of continuing the investigations. This is what many agents considered to be a "goof off or a gold brick." Felt did not have the guts to close worthless cases and so he lied to his superiors and to Hoover about his useless case load. It is what ADIC and Chief Inspector Jimmy "Blue Eyes" Gale referred to as "sustained mediocrity." In my opinion, when Felt was later assigned to work for Gale, Mark Felt learned how to blame other agents for mistakes, but claimed credit for anything that went well, if he could put himself within arm's length of the banana tree.

CHAPTER 49
1971 Break-in of an FBI Office

A case in point.

March 8, 1971, is another day that will live in infamy in the history of the FBI. A handful of political antagonists, who were anti-FBI and anti-Vietnam war, succeeded in breaking into the FBI Resident Agency (RA) office in Media, PA, late at night, and stealing documents about *COINTELPRO* from an ordinary office filing cabinet. Up until that time, the FBI conducted its illegal and unethical *TOP SECRET COINTELPRO* operations against the Old Left, the New Left, the Black Panther Party, White Supremacists, and many other groups the FBI considered radical, unholy and unwanted. Everyone that Hoover, ADIC Gale, and Inspector Felt did not like was on the list of people to be neutralized under *COINTELPRO*.

Oliver "Buck" Revell, who later held the number three position in the FBI, had been a field office supervisor in Philadelphia which covered the Media RA. Revell did not offer any suggestions or direction to the Senior RA as to how to safeguard *COINTELPRO* documents in the Media RA. Why is that?

The collateral damage after the break-in was awesome. Some agents, who were up to their eyeballs in *COINTELPRO* took sick leave not knowing what Mark Felt had planned for their careers or their pensions even though *COINTELPRO* had been approved by top level FBI officials including Hoover, Gale, and Felt. J. Edgar Hoover had never been so embarrassed in his life and so he was out for blood. By then Mark Felt was Hoover's right-hand hatchet man and his Chief Head hunting Inspector for many years. Hoover wanted a body count at Media, PA, and so Felt went looking for heads to chop off. If he had to, Felt could blame a FBI agent for the bad weather anywhere in the country and Hoover would rejoice because Hoover could escape blame and thus not be embarrassed.

Remember now, Mark Felt claims to have become the Chief Inspector in November 1963, just before President Kennedy was assassinated. Felt held that goon squad position for six years. Felt had accused many agents, supervisors, ASACs and SACs of nitpicking mistakes. Many agents were criticized for having a dirty ash tray on top of their desk. Some SACs were censured because the American flag and the State flag were improperly crossed in their offices. Any dim wit knows that the American flag pole, when crossing a state flag pole, should be placed in front of the state flag. However, if a cleaning lady from a third world country does not know any better and she reversed the position of the flags just prior to Felt swooping down from the trees for a surprise inspection, then the SAC would get a letter of censure from Mark Felt while Felt scored humongous brownie points with Hoover.

In my opinion, Mark Felt loved skewering agents on a regular basis to impress Hoover.

If two different size paper clips are in the same bowl on the SAC's desk, then the SAC will receive a letter of censure from Mark Felt saying it is inefficient and time wasting to search for the proper size clip the SAC may want for his notes.

One agent was transferred a thousand miles away for being five pounds overweight. Another agent, with children in school, was transferred from Phoenix to Chicago, in the dead of winter, because the agent had missed a five-day reporting deadline to the United States Attorney on a stolen car case. The rule was not in effect at the time of the delay, but Felt transferred the agent for retroactive disobedience. The inspectors made the rule retroactive and transferred the agent two thousand miles.

Some agents were censured for having pictures of their wives and children locked in their private desks. Some were censured for having travel brochures in their desk for upcoming vacations. Felt censured some agents for having a tooth brush and tooth paste in a locked desk. Others were censured for having a comb or a razor in their locked desks. Boxes containing index cards had to be clearly marked as "Investigative Aides." These are just a few examples of Felt's depleted mentality as an inspector when it came to looking for reasons to censure an agent. Hoover loved Felt's idiotic nit picking in an effort to whip agents into line.

Mark Felt never conducted a criminal investigation in his life and yet he, as the Chief Inspector, was supposed to tell field agents how to handle a criminal investigation.

Now catch this about the RA at Media, PA. Mark Felt and his goon squad inspected hundreds of offices and Resident Agency offices during Felt's tenure as Hoover's chief head hunter. Not once did Felt recommend that top secret COINTELPRO documents be stored in the burglar-proof safes already present in many RAs including the Media Resident Agency office. The Media RA had been inspected every year leading up to March 1971, but not once had Felt said anything about where to keep COINTELPRO documents. Felt would rather focus on paper clips and personal items that agents had inside their locked desks.

There were no written directives in The Manual of Instructions or the Rules and Regulations as to how COINTELPRO documents should be stored in a resident agency. I know because I was the Senior Resident Agent in Paintsville and London, Kentucky for five years. In fact, those two RAs did not have a burglar-proof safe to store any FBI valuables. I had to take all valuable documents, handcuffs and firearms home with me every night because Felt would not supply burglar-proof safes. He thought they were too expensive for Paintsville and London, KY. During my first inspection in Paintsville one of the Inspector's aides focused on different sized note pads left in a cabinet by the former Resident Agent.

However, FBI manuals did state how and where to store two-way radios, Bureau firearms, handcuffs, blackjacks and the National Crime Information Center operation manual. The Senior Resident Agent in Media had followed the directions to the letter. One has to believe that if directions existed in the various manuals of rules and regulations as to how and where to store COINTELPRO documents that the Media, PA SRA would have done so since he complied with all other directives in his office.

During another inspection Mark Felt's team gave me a letter of censure because I had not immediately requested another office to advise the owner of a reported stolen car that the car had been located in Kentucky. The Kentucky State Police determined that the owner of the vehicle had driven it to Kentucky where the owner set fire to the car for insurance purposes. I did not think the FBI needed to waste the taxpayer's money to notify the owner where he burned his car to a crisp. Mark Felt thought otherwise because the Manual of

Instructions stated that owners should be advised immediately when their car is recovered. This is the sort of mind set that was supervising the investigation of the Kennedy assassination. It is no wonder Oswald was proclaimed the lone assassin.

CHAPTER 50
Locking the Barn After the Fact

After the Media burglary Felt wanted to place burglar-proof safes in 475 of the 536 resident agencies. This is much like locking the barn after the horse had been stolen. But, it would have cost approximately $475,000 and so Felt did not give the RAs the needed safes. What the FBI did instead was to place armed guards in the RAs from 5 PM to 8 AM Monday thru Friday and around the clock on Saturdays and Sundays. I know this is true because I acted as one of the armed guards for a week at Palm Springs, California and for two weeks at Santa Barbara, California. Other agents and I were also permitted to claim per diem on those days away from Los Angeles. The guard duty consisted of sleeping on an army cot in the RA office. Our days were free to do what we liked. In Santa Barbara it was usually a day on the beach and an early dinner with cocktails.

Mark Felt was concerned about spending close to $500,000.00 on burglar-proof safes, but he had absolutely no concern about spending several million dollars in agent's salaries, and per diem until the RAs could be retrofitted with burglar alarms wired to the main headquarters offices such as Los Angeles. If an RA were broken into then alarms would go off at the local police station and at the FBI headquarters office in Los Angeles.

Mark Felt was penny wise and pound foolish when it came to solving the problem of security in the hundreds of resident agencies. As Felt writes, the burglar-proof safe at Media went untouched by the burglars, so why did Felt not instruct agents to store COINTELPRO documents in the burglar-proof safe? Because it absolutely did not occur to him that someone might break into an unguarded FBI office.

The many agents who played security guard for countless weeks appreciated Felt's narrow mindedness because we received paid vacations in places like Palm Springs and Santa Barbara. The agents in other field offices had a real blast guarding their respective RAs, but Santa Barbara duty was not half bad at the taxpayer's expense. Thank you, Mr. Felt.

To save money, Felt could have ordered the Santa Barbara agents to guard their own office at night. There were at least five agents in Santa Barbara. They could have taken turns sleeping in their own office and could have saved the taxpayers millions of dollars.

CHAPTER 51
Felt's Response to Media, PA

Felt did his usual hatchet job on field agents when mistakes were made that Felt should have prevented as the Chief Inspector. Because Felt wanted to show Hoover how ruthless he could be and that the Media break-in was not Felt's fault, but the fault of the sustained mediocrity of the senior resident agent, Felt did what he was known best for, attacking subordinates. The rumor spread like wildfire to Los Angeles as to what Felt did. Felt confirms the rumor by writing in his book how he had crucified the Media RA. Felt gleefully writes, "Hoover was enraged, and so was I. The senior resident agent in charge had failed to protect Bureau documents by putting them in the safe, and I recommended stern disciplinary action; he was suspended for a month without pay and given a punitive transfer to the Atlanta field office."

This is how Mark Felt made his mark. No pun intended. It should have been obvious to Felt that resident agencies needed safe places to store COINTELPRO documents. Felt did not recognize the problem because he thought no one would dare break into an FBI office under the cover of darkness. He was more interested it having fun with his wife, whom he took on inspections, against Bureau rules, than he was about his job. No inspector's aide dared to report Felt for violating the rules. If an agent had reported Felt for taking Mrs. Felt on an official inspection trip at the taxpayer's expense, Felt would have suggested to Hoover that that agent be disciplined. If an agent had taken his own wife on an inspection trip Felt would have recommended disciplinary action. It is no wonder that the field agents did not like or respect Felt. The rules applied to others, but not to Mark Felt.

In April 1971, Hoover ordered all FBI field offices to discontinue COINTELPRO. So what did Mark Felt do? Felt built a new barn—installing security systems in all the resident agency offices, which cost millions of dollars. Felt ordered up a temporary guard system while the electronic security systems were being installed. Millions of taxpayer's dollars later the FBI had a great security system for the resident agency offices. The only problem was that all this money had been spent to protect COINTELPRO documents when the COINTELPRO program was being discontinued. What Felt and the FBI had done never made any sense to me. After the horse had been stolen the FBI not only locked the barn, but they built a new barn when they were going out of the horse (COINTELPRO) business. Now that is brilliant!

CHAPTER 52
Felt has his Facts Wrong

I was the FBI's terrorist bombing expert in New York City in 1969 and up to May 1970. Several bombs had been placed in various locations in New York City during 1969 and 1970 by Sam Melville, a member of the Crazies, not the Weathermen, as Felt had claimed.

Mark Felt has some bombings confused with the accidental explosion at the townhouse owned by Mr. and Mrs. Oughton in Greenwich Village on March 6, 1970, which killed Diana Oughton, Ted Gold, and Terry Robins who were Weathermen. One of the townhouses next door was owned by actor Dustin Hoffman, who was not injured. Cathy Wilkerson and Kathy Boudin escaped the explosion unharmed. Kathy Boudin was observed by a neighbor running down the street naked. I had interviewed the neighbor who said she had given Boudin some clothes and then Boudin disappeared down the street.

Mark Felt claims that the Weathermen had exploded bombs all over the United States. It is true that the Weathermen planted a few bombs, but they had not set off nearly as many bombs as the Anti-Castro Cubans who were trained by the CIA in explosives at the JM/Wave training camp in Florida in the early 1960s. The number of bombs set by the CIA trained Anti-Castro Cubans was more than twice the number set off by the Weathermen, but Felt does not even mention the Cubans who were trained by the CIA.

CHAPTER 53
Wrongful Prosecution of Geronimo Pratt

Under Mark Felt's leadership, and Hoover's watchful eye, Elmer Geronimo *"Gi Jaga"* Pratt was sentenced to life behind bars for a murder he did not commit. Then the FBI arranged to keep Pratt in solitary confinement for eight years.

Edward S. Miller and Mark Felt were convicted in 1980 for authorizing illegal break-ins against the Weatherman Underground Organization (WUO). Miller inspected the Los Angeles FBI office in April, 1971. Miller reviewed the Black Panther Party files and permitted the Los Angeles FBI office to withhold information from the court with Felt's approval.

The top leadership of the FBI covered up the many lies told by the FBI in the many appeal motions Pratt had made for habeas corpus. A final hearing was held in 1997 in Orange County, away from Los Angeles where Pratt had been wrongfully convicted. The judge released Pratt pending a new trial. Pratt sued the FBI and the LAPD and was awarded $4.5 million in 2000. This was the case I had so fervently worked on for eighteen years

James Gale, Mark Felt and Edward Miller covered up the wrongful prosecutions in Boston in 1965 where four innocent men were sent to prison for life just to protect an FBI informant. In 2007, this travesty of justice came to light. The judge overseeing the lawsuit case awarded two of the remaining live victims and their families a total of $101 million.

In a different Boston case, Gale, Felt and Miller covered up the prosecution of another innocent man to protect an informant who was a murderer. FBI agent John Connolly went to jail for his part in the cover-up in connection with the Ferme and Whitey Bulger cases.

CHAPTER 54
William F. Roemer Jr. Insults the FBI.

*I*t is my opinion that Roemer committed treason by covering up the Chicago Mob alliance with the CIA and the conspiracy to assassinate President John F. Kennedy.

Before hitting Roemer with a few knock-out blows, I would like to say a few nice things about Bill Roemer, Jr. To my knowledge he never cheated on his wife. He seldom swore. He tried to smoke but that did not pan out even in the 1950s when nearly everyone smoked. He did not know how to drink hard liquor. The strongest drink I ever heard him order was a Shirley Temple. He claims in his book that he drank beer with the Mafia hoods, but I think this is an exaggeration. It was more like he watched the bubbles disappear while letting the beer go flat. Maybe Roemer had learned his lesson when he got drunk at Jim Saine's restaurant on Rush Street. Roemer told me how he had four stingers with Maz Rutland and Ralph Hill. If true, Roemer had gone to an upstairs room to sober up. He undressed and lay down on a couch. Suddenly, he got sick and ran downstairs, through the restaurant filled with customers, to the men's room wearing only his under shorts and T-shirt. This was Hoover's FBI in action. Any other agent would have been fired for pulling such a stunt.

I believe Roemer was a good Christian man. His parting comment to any conversation with anyone, even with the bad guys, was "Keep the faith." I must have heard Roemer say "Keep the faith" thousands of times. I believe Roemer meant what he said because Roemer was able to find some good in everyone, even in murderers such as Sam Giancana, Tony "Joe Batters" Accardo, and Richard Cain.

When William F. Roemer, Jr. decided to anoint Richard Cain as a Special Agent (SA) of the FBI, Roemer insulted every agent past, present, and future. How dare Roemer consider a "made guy" in the Chicago Mafia, and Sam Giancana's right-hand-man, as a Special Agent of the FBI?

How dare Bill Roemer consider anyone a Special Agent of the FBI whom he knows conspired to assassinate President John F. Kennedy? With an insult like that I have no problem landing several knock-out punches to Roemer's credibility. He has asked for it.

In one eulogy written by John J. Flood and published on the Internet, it is reported that J. Edgar Hoover had hand picked Roemer. This is not true. Bill Roemer asked to be assigned to the newly formed C-1 squad also known as the THP squad in Chicago. Roemer wanted to get away from Joseph M. Culkin, his supervisor on Security Squad 4. I overheard Joe Culkin chewing out Roemer's ass more than once for the way he mishandled investigations, according to bureau rules, and because Roemer was spending nearly every afternoon playing handball at a local YMCA on Chicago's Westside. When I heard the rumor that Roemer was spending hours on end of bureau time playing handball I visited the YMCA myself, along with another agent, and there was Roemer playing handball on bureau time. When Roemer saw us he nearly dropped his badge. From then on Roemer was as sweet as pie whenever we met, or had lunch together.

Back in 1957, when Joe Culkin and I were good buddies, Culkin said, "I'd like to fry that bastard's ass but I can't because I'm Catholic and Roemer is a graduate of Notre Dame. Johnny Mohr (who was the ADIC of the Administrative Division at the Bureau) would have *my* ass if I ever criticized Roemer. If Roemer were Protestant his ass would be on the way to Anchorage, Alaska, if not on the way out of the bureau."

A Catholic agent in New York City told me in 1970 that the Catholic click at the Bureau, headed by Johnny Mohr, runs the FBI. I asked, "I thought Hoover ran the FBI?"

Jerry responded, "Hoover has the final say, but it is the Catholic click that makes suggestions to Hoover, which Hoover almost always approves."

I had suspected something like this, but I did not have any proof until told by a Catholic agent that this was the case. I have nothing against Catholics. I don't like favoritism in a bureaucracy toward any religious group.

When Roemer asked for a transfer to the THP squad in 1957, Culkin could not wait to recommend that Roemer be transferred. I had not seen Culkin smile so broadly in years. After Roemer was assigned to C-1 he was still playing handball at the YMCA as late as 1962. This is what some agents termed a "goof off."

CHAPTER 55
Bill Roemer Lost His FBI Credentials

Roemer and I worked on Squad #1 in Chicago, the Infiltration Squad, or the Black Bag Job squad for several years. One day we were preparing to surveill Mollie West, who was the Secretary of the Communist Party of Illinois, a top level position. Mollie West had been on the Security Index and was listed as a Key Figure and a Top functionary. I wrote the first ever Summary Report on Mollie West, which, if I remember correctly was ninety-seven pages.

The day Roemer and I were to follow Mollie; I was intently waiting for a signal that Mollie was leaving her apartment. Roemer was sitting in the passenger side of the car. He began to pat down each pocket. His face turned white as if he had seen a ghost. Then he hopped out of the car and searched under the front seat. He then opened the rear door and searched the back seat pulling out the spring seat. Roemer shouted, "Give me the trunk key!"

I knew immediately what was wrong when Roemer began to pat down every pocket of his clothes. He had lost his FBI credentials, which were in a black leather case. These were the same credentials that one now sees exhibited on various TV shows involving the FBI.

Roemer jumped into the front seat, handed me the keys and shouted, "Let's go back to the office!"

I asked, "What the hell is wrong?"

M. WESLEY SWEARINGEN

Roemer said, "I lost my credentials."

I replied, "Oh, shit."

Roemer picked up the car radio microphone and said to the other agents on the surveillance, "We have to return to the office. We will be back shortly."

One agent chuckled over the radio. Apparently Roemer had lost his credentials while working with that agent.

As I pulled up in front of the FBI office at 212 West Monroe Street, I said, "Go ask the janitor on the other side of the street if he saw a little black case."

I had picked up Roemer across from the office where he had been waiting for me to arrive from the garage before leaving to surveill Mollie West. Roemer had apparently dropped his credentials as he entered the car.

Roemer walked up to the janitor who had been cleaning the sidewalk. I saw him hand Roemer the credentials.

Roemer quickly ran back to the car with a big grin on his face and said, "The janitor said, 'I wondered how long it would take for you to come back for these?' "

Roemer picked up the car radio mike and announced that we were on our way back to Mollie's. We returned to our old position before Mollie left her apartment. All was well with Roemer, once more.

If a member of the communist party had found Roemer's credentials I doubt seriously that even Johnny Mohr could have saved Roemer's career. Hoover would have terminated Roemer then and there in 1955.

Many of us drove when we had Roemer as a partner. We were shocked when Roemer was assigned to the surveillance squad since Roemer had totaled two bureau cars in his first office. Roemer's excuse was that he was not taught how to drive in the FBI Training School. If Roemer had not been a

Notre Dame graduate he most likely would have been fired. Protestant agents were fired by Hoover, with Johnny Mohr's recommendation, for far less blunders.

CHAPTER 56
The Spy That Vanished

A few years later I worked with Roemer on a Russian spy case. Roemer had the ticket on a man some janitor called the office about. The janitor believed the man was a spy because the man stayed in his apartment until about 1 AM. The man would then go out for two or three hours and then return. The man had no means of support other than the woman he was living with in the apartment.

The janitor said the man always paid his bills on time and in cash. One time a doctor came to the apartment to treat the woman's child for a cold but the man refused to let the doctor enter the apartment and so the doctor treated the child in the hallway. The man then paid the doctor in cash.

I suggested to Supervisor Joe Culkin that we set up a late night surveillance and that we use our ultra violet camera to take pictures so as not to alarm the unsub just in case the janitor's suspicions were correct. Culkin liked the idea, but Roemer was not happy about going to work at midnight just to follow someone that a janitor thought was a Russian spy.

We did the surveillance and I took several photographs of the unknown subject, or unsub, with ultra violet light, which could not be seen at night. I became more intrigued by the man's maneuvers because he came out late at night and disappeared down a dark alley. We never saw him come out the other end of the alley only one block away. We did not want to spook the man just in case he might truly be a Russian spy in hiding,

We sent photos to other major offices and asked them to show the photos to top level informants in an effort to identify the unknown subject. After about a month, the Bureau told Chicago to go interview the girl friend and to stop spending so much time on a feeble case.

I was vehemently opposed to interviewing the girl friend until all offices had reported their contacts with informants.

Roemer was too chicken to tell the Bureau to wait for the results from New York City where Jack Childs was a top level informant who had been trained by the KGB.

Culkin sent Roemer and me to interview the girl friend. I told Bill, "Roemer, you are a real dumb ass for interviewing the girl friend before we hear from New York."

Roemer answered, "I'm just following Bureau orders."

"Yeah, and you're possibly going to blow the biggest case you have ever had assigned to you."

"What am I supposed to do? Besides, the janitor is probably paranoid."

"Don't be such a gutless wonder. Wait until we hear from Jack Childs and then you can interview the girlfriend until hell freezes over."

Roemer asked, "Who is Jack Childs?"

"You have never heard of Jack Childs? Do you have your head in the sand, or what? He is the older brother of Morris Childs. Maybe you have heard of CG-5824-S?"

"I have seen the symbol number in reports."

"Well, Morris has a brother in New York who is also an informant. Jack went to the KGB's spy school in the Kremlin."

Roemer said, "I did not know that."

Roemer and I were waiting for the man's girlfriend who worked as a nurse to leave the nearby hospital and walk home to her apartment.

As the nurse departed the hospital, Roemer swiftly walked up to her and flashed his FBI credentials. I did likewise. I had a gut feeling that this was one hell of a blunder. We had spent several nights on surveillance to get photographs of this suspected Russian spy and now Roemer was going to blow everything we had accomplished in one short interview. My position was that we could always interview the girlfriend when all other options have failed.

Roemer asked all the kindergarten questions from the manual of instructions that we learned in training school. The nurse knew next to nothing about her live-in boyfriend. The more she talked the more I knew we had possibly blown one hell of a spy case. Roemer asked the girlfriend not to tell her live-in boyfriend, but it was obviously too late.

A few days later New York sent us the bad news. Just days after Roemer and I interviewed the nurse, the New York Office reported that Jack Childs, who was then NY-4309-S*, identified the photographs of the unknown subject as a former student of the KGB. NY-4309-S* reported that the unknown subject was apparently assigned to an underground post in Chicago. Jack Childs reported that the unsub disappeared after his KGB training in Moscow and Jack had not heard about him until now.

The next day Roemer and I approached the nurse on the street. She immediately broke out crying. I asked, "What's wrong." I had a feeling what was wrong and she confirmed it.

She said, "I told my boyfriend that the FBI had asked me some questions. He got up, packed his private papers, packed some underwear and socks and left the apartment. I have not heard from him since. He didn't take his books, any of his other papers, none of his clothes, or anything. He just disappeared out of my life. I had hopes that we could get married. Now I'm all alone."

I said to Roemer, "Oh, shit, Roemer. You really blew this one, big time."

Roemer said, "It wasn't my fault. It is the Bureau's fault."

"You didn't have to rush out here like the place was on fire and interview the girl friend. You could have waited a few more days to hear from New York"

"The Bureau wanted me to close the case without wasting any more time."

"Hell, you don't waste time by not doing anything. All you had to do was play handball for a few days and wait until New York responded."

"What's done is done."

"When in the hell are you going to learn to be patient?" I asked. "You conduct an investigation like it is a house on fire."

"What do you mean?"

"You go around punching and jabbing at a case like you are still in the boxing ring. When are you going to slow down and methodically investigate a case by piecing it together like a puzzle?"

"Well, I just did what the Bureau told me to do."

"Swell."

I never worked another case with Roemer. I did not want to be a party to his incompetence.

CHAPTER 57
Roemer in Denial

In May of 1960, after Roemer was on the THP squad about two years, I asked him if he knew that the CIA was planning to train Sam Giancana, Johnny Roselli, and Richard Cain how to kill Fidel Castro. Roemer just laughed and said, "Swearingen, don't come to me with crap like that. Since July 29, 1959, we have known everything Giancana and Cain are doing. We know everything that is going on in Chicago. We've got these hoods covered like a blanket. Besides, the CIA doesn't need to train these mob types how to rub out a fink. They are all experts at chopping a guy."

I noticed that Roemer picked up on the mob vernacular such as rub out, hit, clip, whack, or chop for the word kill. Roemer talked about interviewing "made guys" and consiglieries as though they were his best friends and were telling him all about the Mafia. What a joke. Roemer was acting like a little boy in a toy shop. He was beginning to imitate the language of the mobsters he was investigating, which made him feel important. Roemer was a nice man, but he could be very naïve at times.

Roemer previously told me, as well as Ralph Hill having mentioned it, that the conversations over "MO," the bug in Giancana's office, were so badly garbled that they were unintelligible. If conversations were often unintelligible how could the FBI know everything that Giancana and Cain were saying?

Roemer often listened to the recorded conversations. This was okay except for the fact that Roemer did not speak Italian or Spanish. If Roemer did speak these languages then he kept it a secret while he was on Joe Culkin's squad.

Roemer told me that when a storm comes through Chicago their bugs often fail. Sometimes they had to go in and repair the problem and so the FBI was out of touch with what was happening with Giancana and Cain for days or weeks at a time.

Roemer writes in his book (page 149) that "a lot has been written about how the Chicago mob and the CIA formed an alliance to kill Castro. In Chicago we were never able to establish definitely that there was in fact such an alliance." Roemer is flat out lying because I told him of such an alliance, but he refused to believe it because he did not hear it over a bug. Roemer continues to write on page 149, "But the Bureau in Washington gathered information from *Chicago* (emphasis added), New York, Miami, and Los Angeles to support this theory."

How can Roemer deny this Mob alliance with the CIA when four different FBI offices, including Chicago, had reported the information to the Bureau in Washington? Roemer had his head in the sand when it came to other sources reporting on the Chicago mob.

Roemer is telling us, including me, that my information, or Mike Simon's, had made it to the Bureau in Washington. I was the only agent in Chicago who was assigned to the Cuban counterintelligence from 1957 to June 1960, when the CIA began working with the Chicago mob. Ramon, a Cuban exile, is the one who told me in 1960 of the coming Bay of Pigs invasion planned for 1961.

Understandably, Roemer and Ralph Hill laughed about the Bay of Pigs when I told them. I myself thought Ramon was off his rocker. None of us in the FBI dreamed that the

CIA could be as stupid, or incompetent, as to plan an invasion of Cuba at the Bay of Pigs, or the assassination of President Kennedy. As it turned out the CIA planned the Bay of Pigs debacle. The assassination of President John F. Kennedy was orchestrated to perfection.

CHAPTER 58
Roemer Admits to the Mafia/CIA Alliance.

In the fall of 1961, and all of 1962, I bombarded Roemer and Hill with information about the CIA and the Chicago mob alliance. In the summer of 1962, Roemer and Hill were informed by me that the Chicago and Florida mobs, and the CIA, were plotting to assassinate President Kennedy. They thought I was nuts. So did my supervisor, Joseph M. Culkin.

Hoover, under the pretext that my new wife Paula was a security risk, had transferred me to Louisville, Kentucky as of January 1, 1963. We had been married on November 21, 1962.

The FBI made available FOIA documents after I retired indicating that Paula and her family were investigated and that she was declared _not_ to be a security risk. Why then was I transferred to Louisville and then three months later to Paintsville, Kentucky? The reason given to me was that Paula, my new bride, was a security risk because she had supported the former Vice President Henry Wallace when he ran for President in 1948, some fourteen years earlier. In essence I could not be trusted not to tell my new wife about my FBI work. The only logical reason for the transfer to such an isolated area as Paintsville is that the Chicago office and Hoover wanted me to stop reporting that the CIA was organizing a conspiracy with the Chicago mob to assassinate President John F. Kennedy.

Roemer claims that he soon learned why Giancana was so knowledgeable about Cuba. Roemer confirms in his book that he learned from other sources, quite possibly me, that Johnny Roselli had been approached by Bob Matheu, the former FBI agent who had worked for Howard Hughes and was now acting for the CIA. Roemer now claims that Giancana had put the CIA in touch with Santo Trafficante, the big boss in Tampa, Florida, whom Giancana had known from the days in Cuba. Roemer admits in his book that Roselli, Giancana, and Trafficante worked in concert with the CIA.

I told Roemer in 1962 that Giancana was in a conspiracy with the CIA and Trafficante to kill Kennedy. Roemer did not want to hear this and did not want to believe it because he had not heard it over a bug or an electronic surveillance (Elsur) such as "MO."

Roemer was so naïve that he thought Giancana and Cain would talk over a bug that they were plotting to kill Kennedy in a conspiracy with the CIA. How stupid can one be?

Roemer claims that Giancana was not serious about going after Castro. Roemer believed Giancana was just playing along with the CIA. Roemer claims that "MO" furnished information indicating that if Giancana made a commitment to help put Kennedy in the White House that Frank Sinatra could get Kennedy to back off from the FBI investigation of Giancana. If Roemer is correct, and I believe he is on this one point, when Bobby Kennedy as the new Attorney General targeted Sam Giancana, then Giancana went along with Roselli, Trafficante, and the CIA to hit President Kennedy.

Roemer told me at least a dozen times about his confrontation with Sam Giancana at the airport. Roemer bragged about how he harassed the hell out of Giancana in front of his girl friend, Phyllis McGuire of the McGuire Sisters Singing Trio, and the general public. Roemer harassed Giancana so badly that Roemer's superior told him to knock it off. Roemer told that story to others in my presence. He was like a little boy talking about his first adventure into the outdoors. The way Roemer bragged about his exploits I thought that Giancana was assigned to him until one day Ralph Hill told me that he had the assignment card on Giancana not Roemer, which Roemer refers to as "the ticket." I began to realize that Roemer was becoming a braggart and taking credit for the exploits of his fellow agents.

Roemer claims in his book that he installed bugs in Giancana's offices, but I knew Roemer and he was all thumbs. When he was on the bag job squad other agents and I requested that he stay outside to avoid wrecking the place. Roemer was like a bull in a china shop when it came to searching through personal papers and notes. The agent who installed the bugs was bureau trained in electronics and had gone to the FBI's Sound School. Roemer never set foot in Sound School as of 1962 when he bragged about bugging Giancana. The agent who installed the bugs was nicknamed "Moose." The other sound man was Pete, who was one of the best in the business.

Moose was the one who installed the bugs in the Polish Consulate in 1959 and they were all found by the Soviet Sweepers. Apparently Roemer was not aware that the Polish Consulate had been swept clean and that every bug was found. This alone should have made Roemer suspicious of what he was hearing over "MO."

Richard Cain was an expert in electronics and the planting of bugs. He most likely swept Giancana's offices and found the FBI bugs, but left them intact so as to obtain feedback from the FBI when agents interviewed the various mobsters. By leaving the bugs where they were planted, Cain, Giancana, and other mobsters, could feed the FBI misinformation. This is what I would have done had I been Richard Cain and from what Roemer writes about Cain; Cain was smarter than the whole THP squad combined.

CHAPTER 59
Roemer's One-man Surveillance.

Roemer's surveillance techniques also left a lot to be desired when he worked on the bag job squad. We agents often had to tell Roemer to back off for fear he would get burned and jeopardize an operation.

An example of Roemer's ineptness on surveillance is the time he attempted to follow mobster Gussie Alex and was burned within six blocks. Roemer was alone on what Roemer called the "surveillance." This was Roemer's first mistake. When following a communist party member we seldom had less than four cars. Soon after Roemer started his surveillance of Alex, Alex had pulled over after he turned the corner. Roemer should not have driven beyond Alex, but he did, and then he parked. This was mistake number two.

Alex drove up behind Roemer, parked, and wrote down the license plate. Alex ran the number through a friend in the Cook County Sheriff's office. This set off alarms in Springfield that someone was running the number on a car secretly registered to the FBI. The SAC in Springfield was alerted. He called the SAC in Chicago. The SAC in Chicago called Roemer in off the street and chewed Roemer's ass out. Any other agent would have been transferred for pulling such a stunt, but Roemer was a Notre Dame graduate and he had protection from the Pope at the Bureau, Johnny Mohr.

The shocker in this event is that Gussie Alex had never before been surveilled by the FBI. Roemer blew the surveillance in less than five minutes. Roemer completely ignored the lessons he had learned on the bag job squad, but Roemer thought he was going to show his colleagues how to conduct a one-man surveillance. Roemer obviously forgot everything he had learned about surveillance in training school. When Alex pulled over and parked, this should have been a clue to Roemer that Alex was on to his antics. Roemer should have driven off and should have come back another day with backup. Roemer blew it big time and his ineptness was the laughter of the office.

Now that Gussie Alex had the license number to the bureau car Roemer used it meant that the car had to be re–registered to another fictitious person to protect the FBI's identity. Also, that particular car could never be used on the surveillance of anyone in the Chicago Mob.

Roemer had been in the FBI nearly eight years and should have known better. Instead, Roemer was still acting like a First Office agent. Nice going, Roemer.

With fifteen years in the FBI and a grade GS-13, Roemer was still acting like a First Office agent when he attempted to get Bernie Glickman to turn state's evidence. Glickman had information about Mob fixes in the boxing arena. What Glickman knew would have blown the lid off the big time boxing matches in Chicago and New York. Roemer screwed up the interview with Glickman so badly that Glickman, at one point during the interview, said to Roemer, "For Christ sake. Am I dealing with some fucking novices here?"

Somehow word leaked out that Glickman talked to the FBI and someone beat the crap out of Glickman. Roemer goofed again, big time.

Then, when it came time for Glickman to be a witness, Roemer let the Department of Justice (DOJ) take over Glickman. After U.S. Attorney Ed Hanrahan heard Glickman's story coupled with the fact that Glickman refused to testify against Tony "Joe Batters" Accardo, which was part of the deal Roemer made with Glickman, Hanrahan washed his hands of Bernie Glickman. Roemer blew it once more and let an informant go to hell. Roemer violated another bureau rule—never throw your informant to the wolves and never let your informant be controlled by the DOJ.

I find it interesting that Bill Roemer believes that when a witness, who is a mobster, a killer, and a hit man for the Mafia, testifies against a Capo, or under boss, that this person is to be believed 100 percent. However, when a private citizen without an arrest record testifies, he or she is not to be believed unless there is some corroborating evidence. Why do individuals like Roemer believe a witness who testifies against a mobster, but that same person is not to be believed when they testify against a government agent, or a law enforcement officer?

In my opinion, William F. Roemer, Jr. committed treason by covering up the CIA's plot to assassinate President Kennedy. Roemer admits in his book that he knew of an alliance between the Chicago mob and the CIA, but that he could never prove it. Roemer claimed that the Warren Commission was told of the association by Lenny Patrick, a known mob killer, with Jack Ruby before Ruby left Chicago. The Warren Commission claimed there was no connection between the Chicago Mob, or Mafia, and Jack Ruby. Did Roemer tell the Warren Commission that he knew of an alliance between the Chicago mob and the CIA, but that he could not prove it?

CHAPTER 60
Roemer could have prevented JFK's death

William F. Roemer Jr. wrote a book which he titled *ROEMER: MAN AGAINST THE MOB*. It would have been nice had Roemer listened to Ramon from 1960 to October 1962. If Roemer had believed my informant instead of what he heard scrambled over the FBI bugs, it is quite possible the FBI may just have been able to stop a handful of rogue CIA agents from assassinating President John F. Kennedy. We will never know because the man who claims to have been "against the mob" never gave it as much as the "old college-try."

I cannot and will not forgive Roemer for not at least listening to what Ramon had to say about the CIA and the Chicago mob. Roemer could have confronted his THP sources. Roemer could have asked Sam Giancana at the airport in 1961 what he was doing training with the CIA to kill Fidel Castro. Roemer could have asked Richard Cain what he (Cain) was doing training Cubans in Florida.

Roemer enjoyed harassing the Chicago mob. Why didn't Roemer spread the word that the Chicago mob was planning to assassinate President Kennedy? Whether Roemer believed Ramon or not, Roemer could have talked up the planned assassination. Maybe that would have put a fire under the U.S. Secret Service to be more alert?

Roemer could have spread the word that the FBI was watching the Mob's every move. Roemer could have called the CIA and said that he was aware that the CIA was working with Giancana, Roselli, and Cain in Florida.

Roemer writes in his book about how he had an "in person" conference with Bobby Kennedy. Roemer could have called Bobby Kennedy and could have told Bobby that he had received reliable information that the CIA, the Chicago Mob, and the Anti-Castro Cubans were planning to assassinate President Kennedy. If Roemer had been as aggressive toward the Chicago Mob about Kennedy as he portrays himself in his book toward the Mob, he could have brought the planned assassination of President Kennedy to a screeching halt.

I had told Roemer what was being planned. If I had had the contacts in the Chicago mob, I would have spread the word myself. I did what I could to inform the agents working the THP gangsters. I was not allowed to contact hoodlums like Giancana, Roselli, or Cain. To the contrary, I would have been severely disciplined if I had talked to these individuals. I had to get Bureau permission to personally hand over photographs to the CIA in Chicago of Russian ships in Cuban waters that had been taken by one of my sources.

As it was, I was transferred out of Chicago because I continued to broach the subject that President Kennedy was the subject of an assassination plot by the CIA, the Chicago Mob, and the Anti-Castro Cubans.

CHAPTER 61
Millie McGhee Morris, Hoover's Black Cousin

Soon after my book, *FBI SECRETS, An Agent's Exposé* had been published in 1995, by South End Press, Boston, Massachusetts; I received a telephone call from a woman identifying herself as Millie McGhee. She said she had grown up on a plantation in Mississippi and that she was a cousin to FBI Director J. Edgar Hoover. I recognized her African-American Mississippi plantation accent since I had worked in Mississippi in 1951-52.

My first impression was that authors receive such calls when a new book is published. At first, Millie's story sounded as though she was in need of professional mental help, which I could not offer. As Millie related to me her childhood nightmare of being told by her grandfather that she was related to the late FBI Director J. Edgar Hoover, but that she should never tell anyone for fear of their house being burned down, or worse still, their family being killed, I began to think Millie just might be able to confirm what Agent Joseph had told me in 1951 about J. Edgar Hoover's biological father being a black man from Mississippi. Instead of brushing Millie off as a basket case, I encouraged her to investigate what she had been told by her grandfather "Big Daddy."

Millie McGhee corresponded with me for many years concerning her progress in searching records, interviewing relatives, and looking at grave markers. Each time she told me of some progress, which she thought may be the answer I informed her that if Hoover were still alive he would crucify her with the limited information she had developed. She needed more confirmation.

Each time Millie came up with new information I told her she had to develop more iron clad evidence that Hoover's father was black, or else her critics and the FBI would have her for lunch. There were times when I was extremely tough on Millie. The more I criticized her work the more it encouraged her to uncover Hoover's dark secret. When Millie finally developed the information she needed to tell her true childhood story, I was behind her one hundred percent.

Millie L. McGhee has written a book titled *What's Done In The Dark*. It was published in 2005 by Inland Empire Services/ Allen-Morris Publishing, located in Rancho Cucamonga, CA.

Millie has done an excellent job of uncovering the facts surrounding her childhood and developing the oral history to document and to prove J. Edgar Hoover's lineage. Millie has even received the backing of Hoover's white relatives.

To quote the cover of Millie's book, "This research uncovers a three hundred year old family secret that is compelling and, to some, shocking."

"The compelling part is the fact that J. Edgar Hoover, one of the Nation's most hated, feared, and (by some) adored men possessed the blood of the very people he ostracized and despised most—Blacks. Mrs. McGhee reveals to the world the shocking truth of how her own African American lineage intersects with that of the former FBI Director J. Edgar Hoover."

I encourage everyone wanting an insight into why J. Edgar Hoover became America's most notorious racist to read and find the answer in Millie McGhee's book *What's Done In The Dark*.

EPILOGUE

It is my opinion that top FBI officials are guilty of treason because they have covered-up the truth behind the assassination of President John F. Kennedy.

James P. Hosty, Jr. writes in his book *Assignment: Oswald*, Arcade Publishing, 1996, that Lee Harvey Oswald was not his informant. This does not mean that Oswald was not someone else's informant.

The FBI wants us to believe that Lee Harvey Oswald traveled to Russia, Oswald publicly supported Fidel Castro in New Orleans by handing out Fair Play For Cuba Committee flyers and leaflets, and Oswald attempted to kill Major General Walker in April 1963 in Dallas and yet the FBI did not so much as interview Oswald until Kennedy was killed? Give me a break folks.

In 1972, Elmer Geronimo Pratt was wrongfully imprisoned because the FBI withheld information from the court that a witness against Pratt was an FBI informant. Because of my eighteen year effort, Pratt was finally released in 1997. Pratt sued the FBI and won an award of $4.5 million in 2000.

The Select Committee on Assassinations concluded in 1979 that the FBI failed to investigate adequately the possibility of a conspiracy to assassinate the President.

Judy Bari was injured when her car was bombed in 1990. Bari sued the FBI, but died in 1997 from her injuries before the court ruled that the FBI and the Oakland Police must pay $4.4 million in damages.

In 2000, Ex-FBI agent John Connolly was prosecuted for protecting his informant Billy "Whitey" Bulger while Bulger killed off the Italian Mafia in Boston. Bulger is now on the FBI's Ten Most Wanted list.

In November 2003, the House Committee on Government Reform charged that the 40-year history of the FBI's organized-crime informant program in New England was "one of the greatest failures in the history of federal law enforcement."

The congressional committee stated that FBI agents became corrupt, encouraged perjury in death cases, let innocent men languish and die in prison, and allowed people to be murdered, all in the name of protecting informants.

The report states, "The results of the committee's investigation make clear that the FBI must improve management of its informant programs to ensure that agents are not corrupted."

The Office of the Inspector General began investigating the FBI Laboratory in 1995, only after agent Frederic Whitehurst brought allegations of corruption. William C. Sullivan called the FBI Laboratory "a real-life counterpart of the busy workroom of the Wizard of OZ—all illusion. Even the famous laboratory files were maintained for show."

The case against former Chicago cop, Steve Manning, was overturned after fourteen years on death row. Manning was released in 2000 after investigation revealed that the FBI had mishandled yet another case.

In 2007, US District Judge Nancy Gertner said that the FBI had deliberately withheld evidence in a 1965 murder conviction which sent four innocent men to prison. Two of the men died behind bars.

Judge Gertner said, "FBI officials up the line allowed their employees to break laws, violate rules, and ruin lives." Judge

Gertner ordered the FBI to pay $101.7 million for the false murder convictions, which is believed to be the largest of its kind.

Oliver "Buck" Revell writes in his book, page 372, about the Kennedy assassination: "I certainly wished that I could have found even a scintilla of evidence that the worst political crime in our nation's history was a conspiracy. Such a revelation would have made me the most celebrated detective since Sherlock Holmes."

Jack Martin, an employee of Guy Bannister, told the FBI in New Orleans that Guy Bannister was involved with the CIA in Kennedy's assassination. This is evidence of a conspiracy even if nothing else had come out about a conspiracy.

Two CIA agents John Garret Underhill and Maurice Brooks Gatlin, Sr. were both killed in May 1964 because they claimed that the CIA was involved in a conspiracy to kill Kennedy. CIA agent David Sanchez Morales stated publicly while referring to President Kennedy that "We took care of that son of a bitch, didn't we?" Morales died of a heart attack in 1978 at the age of 52 soon after his public outburst. He was building a new home in Arizona.

Knowing what we now know about how the FBI protects informants, I have no doubt that Carlos Marcello was a Top Hoodlum Program informant just as Richard Cain was a THP informant in Chicago. Bill Roemer protected Cain. When former FBI agent Regis Kennedy testified before the Select Committee on Assassinations he said that Carlos Marcello was nothing more than a "tomato salesman and a real estate investor." Regis Kennedy was either mentally retarded, or he was protecting Marcello as an FBI informant pure and simple.

Former Secret Service agent, Abraham Bolden, has written a new book entitled *The Echo from Dealey Plaza,* Harmony

Books, New York, 2008. Bolden writes about the cover-up by Secret Service of reports that anti-Castro Cubans were allegedly plotting to assassinate the president.

I rest my case.
Now you, the reader, make your decision.

GLOSSARY

ADD   Associate Deputy Director

ADIC   Assistant Director in Charge

AG   Attorney General of the United States

AIRTEL   A written memorandum between FBI field offices or Bureau headquarters. It is a 1950s acronym for a memo sent via air mail in teletype format. Over the years it became bastardized into the usual verbose bureaucratic memo as opposed to the short and abrupt teletype format. The AIRTEL was originally created to save money; however, it still requires the immediate handling of investigative leads and the immediate distribution by the clerical staff to the intended receiver.

Apalachin   The turning point in the FBI's investigation of the American Mafia. The largest ever known meeting of mobsters took place in 1957 in Apalachin, New York, which was discovered accidentally by a New York State Police Trooper. This huge discovery embarrassed Hoover's FBI into finally investigating organized crime.

ASAC   Assistant Special Agent in Charge of an FBI Field Office.

AUSA   Assistant United States Attorney.

Bill Roemer	William F. Roemer, Jr. thought he was the FBI's greatest crime fighter. Roemer wrote a self aggrandizing book titled *Roemer: Man Against the Mob*. Roemer also wrote a book placing Chicago's former mob boss, Tony Accardo, on a pedestal.
Black Bag Job	The FBI's term for an illegal search. The term originated from the use of a black leather bag to carry lock picking tools, cameras, steamers, letter openers, flashlights, and other equipment to conduct an illegal search after picking a lock.
Brick Agent	Agents who work in the field offices conducting investigations.
Bureau	The term used by FBI Field Agents when referring to FBI headquarters in Washington, D.C., also known as FBIHQ
Bug	A hidden microphone placed in an office or private residence, which is different from a wire tap on a telephone, often done without a court order or Attorney General approval making the information inadmissible in court.
C-1	The FBI's Criminal Squad Number One in Chicago, which handled the investigation of organized crime also known as the Top Hoodlum Program (THP) squad.
CIA "asset"	An informant, a source, or assassin used by the CIA, but is not a government employee.
"Chop"	To kill.

"Clip"   To murder gangland style.

COINTELPRO The FBI's code word for the counter-intelligence program, which was in operation from the mid-1950s until April 21, 1971. COINTELPRO continued under individual case titles such as Judy Bari.

Consiglieri   A highly placed advisor or counselor in an organized crime family. Tony Accardo had been the Consiglieri in Chicago after handing over the position of absolute boss to Sam Giancana in 1957.

DAD   Deputy Associate Director

"Dry Clean"   To take evasive action to detect a physical surveillance. This is what Gus Alex did the first day Bill Roemer followed Alex and Alex immediately made Roemer's B movie surveillance.

"ELSUR"   The FBI's code word for electronic surveillance in the form of a bug or a wiretap.

FBIHQ   FBI Headquarters in Washington D.C.

"FISUR"   The FBI's code word for physical surveillance.

"Hit"   To kill.

La Cosa
Nostra -
(LCN)   La Cosa Nostra was the term given to organized crime families by law enforcement to romanticize the mob.

"Loop"   The downtown area of Chicago originally surrounded by the elevated train tracks also called "The Loop.".

"Made Guy"   An actual member of the Chicago's LCN mob family. Richard Cain was a made guy working for Sam Giancana, also a Chicago Cop, a CIA asset, and a FBI informant. Bill Roemer naively considered Cain to be a Special Agent of the FBI.

"MO"	The FBI's bug placed in Sam Giancana's office in Chicago.
SAC	Special Agent in Charge of a field office.
"Rub Out"	To kill.
Tap	A wire-tap usually placed on a telephone through the telephone company with a court order, or with approval from the Attorney General
THP	Top Hoodlum Program.
"Whack"	To kill.

A SPECIAL AWARD

The California Attorneys For Criminal Justice honored me with the President's Award on December 13, 1997.

"It is with great pride that
CALIFORNIA ATTORNEYS FOR CRIMINAL JUSTICE
Presents the
PRESIDENT'S AWARD
To
WES SWEARINGEN
For your Courage, Commitment, Unswerving Faith, and United Effort to Overcome Racism, Oppression and Injustice and Win Freedom for Geronimo Ji Jaga Pratt.
President: Marcia A. Morrissey
December 13, 1997

In 1972, and for nearly twenty-five years, top officials of the FBI covered-up the fact that the FBI had withheld evidence from the California courts in an effort to put and to keep Geronimo Pratt, an innocent man, in prison.

If top FBI officials such as J. Edgar Hoover, Clarence M. Kelley, William H. Webster, Louis Freeh, W. Mark Felt and Oliver "Buck" Revell could cover up the imprisonment of an innocent man for twenty-five years, then there is no question that they can cover-up FBI and CIA wrongdoing in the assassination of President John F. Kennedy

INDEX

A

Accardo, Tony 44-45, 193, 228, 249, 260-261

Adams, James B. 71

Adler Planetarium 53

AFT 200

Agent Joseph 5-10, 253

Air France 116

AIRTEL 116, 259

Alex, Gus 12, 247-248

Alliance of Theatrical Stage Employees 28

Alpha 66 61, 115, 131

Anderson, Jack 32, 198

Anti-Castro Cuban 11, 62, 81, 115, 223, 252, 258

Apalachin, NY 12, 105, 152, 259

Artime, Manuel 61-62, 69, Contents

ATF 200

Atlas, Charles 153

Assignment: Oswald by James Hosty, Jr. 92,185,255

B

Baby-Face Nelson 6

Baker, Bobby 152, 156-157

Bannister, Guy, aka. Banister 65-67, 69, 111-112, 146, 157-158, 172, 178-180, 182, 257

Bari, Judy 255, 261, Introduction

H

"Kiss Me Deadly," 101
Koethe, James F. 146, 180
Kupcinet, Irv 145, 176
Kupcinet, Karyn 145, 176

L
La Cosa Nostra (LCN) 12, 30, 261
Lake Lugert 144, 176
Lake Shore Drive 44, 47, 49, 51, 101, 107, 141
Las Vegas 27-29, 51, 55, 112, 141-142, 147, 157,
    Contents
Lightfoot, Claude 119
Linberg, Elmer 164
Lincoln, President Abraham 96
Lincoln Convertible 195
Linguaphone Institute 14
Lode, Jake 150-173
Long Beach Police Department 145, 178
Los Angeles Police Department (LAPD) 116,137, 225,
    Introduction
Louisville 71-72, 76, 80-83, 85-87, 91, 95, 111-112, 115,
    243, Contents
Los Subversivos 117

M
Machine-Gun Kelly 6
Mafia 1-2, 8, 11-12, 15-16, 24-25, 29-32, 38-39, 42, 44,
    47-48, 52, 54-55, 57-60, 66-67, 71, 77, 81-82, 95, 98,
    101, 105, 112-113, 131-135, 150-152, 156-157, 159,
    162, 170-171, 182, 185, 187-188, 192, 195, 198, 227-228,
    239, 243, 249, 256, 259, Contents
Maheu, Robert "Bob" 27-29